THE ADVENTURES OF
THE U-202

THE ADVENTURES OF THE U-202 SUBMARINE

AN ACTUAL NARRATIVE

BY

BARON SPIEGEL VON UND ZU PECKELSHEIM
(CAPTAIN-LIEUTENANT, COMMANDER OF THE U-202)

**Fredonia Books
Amsterdam, The Netherlands**

The Adventures of the U - 202 Submarine:
An Actual Narrative

by
Baron Spiegel von Und Zu Peckelsheim

ISBN: 1-4101-0349-8

Copyright © 2003 by Fredonia Books

Reprinted from the 1917 edition

Fredonia Books
Amsterdam, The Netherlands
http://www.fredoniabooks.com

All rights reserved, including the right to reproduce this book, or portions thereof, in any form.

In order to make original editions of historical works available to scholars at an economical price, this facsimile of the original edition of 1917 is reproduced from the best available copy and has been digitally enhanced to improve legibility, but the text remains unaltered to retain historical authenticity.

PREFACE

I WAS sitting on the conning tower smoking a cigarette. Then the splash of a wave soaked it. I tried to draw another puff. It tasted loathsome and frizzled. Then I became angry and threw it away.

I can see my reader's surprised expression. You had expected to read a serious U-boat story and now such a ridiculous beginning! But I know what I am doing. If I had once thrown myself into the complicated U-boat system and used a bunch of technical terms, this story would be shorter and more quickly read through, but you would not have understood half of it.

Seriousness will come, bitter and piti-

PREFACE

able seriousness. In fact, everything is serious which is connected with the life on board a submarine and none of it is funny; although in fact it is the hundred small inconveniences and peculiar conditions on a U-boat which make life on it remarkably characteristic. And in order to bring to the public a closer knowledge concerning the peculiar life on board a U-boat I am writing this story. Good—therefore my logbook! Yes, why should I not make use of it? To this I also wish to add that I not only used my own log-book but also at many places had use of other U-boats' logs in order to present one or another episode which is worth the while relating. Thus, for example, the story of the many fishing-smacks, which are spoken of in the chapter called "Rich Spoils," is borrowed, but the hap-

PREFACE

penings in the witch kettle, the adventure with the English bulldog, and also most of the other chapters are my own feathers with which I have adorned this little story. This is the only liberal right of an author which I permit myself. The style of the story from a logbook is simple and convenient, and one buys so willingly such stories. See there two valid reasons for making use of it.

THE AUTHOR.

CONTENTS

CHAPTER		PAGE
I	OUR FIRST SUCCESS	3
II	AN EVENTFUL NIGHT	21
III	THE SINKING OF THE TRANSPORT	46
IV	RICH SPOILS	68
V	THE WITCH-KETTLE	91
VI	A DAY OF TERROR	115
VII	A LIVELY CHASE	140
VIII	THE BRITISH BULL-DOG	163
IX	HOMEWARD BOUND!	189

THE ADVENTURES OF THE
U-202

THE ADVENTURES OF THE U-202

I

OUR FIRST SUCCESS

At the hunting grounds North Sea, April 12, 19—Course: northwest. Wind: southwest, strength 3-4. Sea: strength 3. View: good. Both machines in high speed.

WE were very comfortable in the conning tower because the weather was fine and the sun burned with its heat our field-gray skin jackets.

"Soon we will have summer," I said to the officer on guard, Lieutenant Petersen, who was sitting with me on the conning tower's platform. I felt entirely too hot in my thick underwear.

Petersen, who, like me, was sitting with his legs dangling in the open hatch on whose edge we had placed ourselves, put his hand on the deck and loosened the thick, camel's wool scarf, twice wrapped around his neck, as if suddenly he realized it was too hot for him, too.

"I think I'll soon discharge this one from service," said Petersen, and pulled at the faithful winter friend as if he wished to strip it off.

"Don't be too hasty, my dear lieutenant," I replied laughing. "Just wait until to-night, and then I am sure that you will repent and take your faithful friend back into the service."

"Are we going to keep above the water to-night, Herr Captain-Lieutenant, or are we to submerge?" he asked me.

OUR FIRST SUCCESS

"It depends on what comes up," I answered. "It rests as usual with the weather."

Thus we were talking and smoking on the conning tower while our eyes scanned the horizon and kept a sharp lookout all around us.

On the little platform, which in a sharp angle triangle unites itself from behind with the tower, the subordinate officer corporal was on guard, and with a skin cloth was cleaning the lenses on his double spy-glass, which were wet.

"Did you also get a dousing, Krappohl?" I asked. "Then you didn't look out, either. That rascal soaked my cigarette just as he did the lenses on your spy-glass. That's the dickens of a trick."

With the word "rascal" I meant the splashing wave, which, while the sea was in a perfect calm, without any reason climbed up to us on the tower. If there had been a storm it would have been nothing to mention. Then we often did not have a dry thread on our bodies. But such a shameless scoundrel, which in the midst of the most beautiful weather suddenly throws himself over a person, is something to make one angry.

We made good speed. The water, which was thrown aside by the bow, passed by us in two wide white formed streaks. The motor rattled and rumbled, and the ventilation machine in the so-called "Centrale" right under our feet made a monotonous buzzing. Through the only opening where the air could pass out, the open tower hatch, all kinds of odors flowed one after another from the lower regions right by our noses. First we smelled smear-oil.

OUR FIRST SUCCESS

Then the fragrance of oranges (we had with us a large shipment, which we had received as a gift of love), and now—ah! Now it was coffee, a strong aromatic coffee odor.

Lieutenant Petersen moved back and forth unrestingly on the "swimwest," with which he had tried to make it a little more comfortable for himself on the hard sitting place, bent deeper and deeper down into the hatch inhaling with greed the odor from below, and said, as he in pleasant anticipation began to rub his hands together:

"Now we'll have coffee, Herr Captain-Lieutenant!"

I had just with a great deal of trouble pulled out a cigarette-case from the inside pocket of my skin jacket and was groping in my other pockets for matches, when a hand (the gloves number 9½) with outstretched forefinger reached towards me from behind and the subordinate officer's excited voice announced:

"A cloud of smoke four points port."

As quickly as lightning the spy-glass was placed to the eye. "Where? Oh, yes, there. I can see it!"

"As yet, only smoke can be seen. Isn't it so?"

In what a suspense we were now. Leaning forward, and with the glasses pressed to the eye, we gazed on the little, distant, cloud of smoke. It curled, then bent with the wind and slowly dissolved in a long, thin veil-like streak. Nothing but smoke could be seen, a sign that the air was clear, and one could see all the way to the extreme horizon.

OUR FIRST SUCCESS

What kind of a ship could it be, which the curved form of the earth still concealed from our view? Was it a harmless freighter, a proud passenger steamer, an auxiliary cruiser, or maybe an armored cruiser jammed with cannon?

It was with a feeling, wavering between hope and fear, that these thoughts occupied my mind—fear, not for the enemy, because we were anxious to meet him—but fear that a disappointment would fall on us, if the ship proved to be a neutral steamer when it came closer. Seven times we had during three days experienced such disappointment, seven times we had met neutral ships without contraband on board, and had been compelled to let them continue on their way.

The distance between us and the

steamer had not diminished, so that its masts and a funnel arose above the horizon, two narrow, somewhat slanting lines, between which there was a thicker dark spot. A common freighter, therefore. This we saw at the first glance. I changed our course northwardly in order to head off the course of the steamer which was going in an easterly direction. With the highest speed the machine could make we raced to meet them and the bridge and part of the hull could already be seen.

"To the diving stations! Artillery alarm. Cannon service on deck! First torpedo tube ready for fire!"

With loud voice I called down these commands into the boat.

There was a stir in the passages below like when a stone is thrown into the midst of a swarm of bees. From

OUR FIRST SUCCESS

below it arose, and the men who were to serve at the cannons crowded on the narrow precipitous ladder, swung themselves through the tower hatch and leaped on the deck. Now, first, just once, a deep breath, so that the lungs can draw the refreshing sea air, and then with their sleeves turned up and flashing eyes to the guns.

"Can you see any neutral signs, Petersen?"

"No, Herr Captain-Lieutenant. The entire hull is black. It's an Englishman."

"The flag of war to the mast! The usual signals ready!" I called down into the tower.

Immediately our flag of war floated from the top of the mast behind the tower. It told the men over there: "Here am I, a German submarine

U-boat. Now for it, you proud Britisher! Now it will be seen who rules the sea."

We had gradually drawn closer to a distance of about six thousand meters. At last an enemy! After so many neutral steamers. At last an enemy! An intense joy thrilled us, a joy which only can be compared with the hunter's when he sees at last the longed-for prey coming within range, after long and fruitless efforts. We had traveled many hundred sea miles. We had endured storm, cold, and at times had been drenched to the skin, and there, only two points port, our first success was waving towards us!

By this time we must have been discovered by the steamer. Now our flag of war must have been recognized. A ghastly horror must have seized the cap-

OUR FIRST SUCCESS

tain on the bridge: The U-boat terror! the U-boat pest!

But the captain on the steamer did not give in so easily. He tried to save himself by flight. Suddenly we saw how the steamer belched forth thicker and darker clouds of smoke and in a sharp curve turned port. Its propeller water, which hitherto could hardly be seen, was whipped to a white foam, and let us know the machines had been put into the highest possible speed. But it was of no use. No matter how much the captain was shouting and how much the machinist drove his sweating and naked fire crew to even more than human endeavors, so that the coal flew about and the boilers were red, everything was useless. We closed in on him with a horrible certainty nearer and nearer.

For some time I had been standing high up on the tower with a spy-glass before my eyes and did not lose one of the steamer's motions. Now it seemed to me the right moment had come to energetically command the steamer to stop.

"A shot above the steamer! Fire!"

The granite landed two hundred meters in front of the steamer. We waited a few minutes, but when the shot did not cause any change I gave the right distance to the gunners and shouted the command to aim at the steamer. The second shot hit and a thick, black and yellow cloud from the explosion shot into the air. The third shot tore a piece off the funnel, the fourth hit the bridge, and before the fifth had left the mouth of the gun the signal flew up, "I have stopped."

OUR FIRST SUCCESS

Ah! old friend, you had come to it, anyhow!

An old sea-rule says: "Carefulness is the best seamanship." Regarding all the tricks and subterfuges which the hostile merchant-marine has used against us, I did not consider it advisable to advance nearer the steamer at once. I therefore also stopped our machines and signaled: "Leave the ship immediately!"

The signal was unnecessary. The English captain had himself given the command to the crew to take to the boats after he, frothing with anger, had comprehended the impossibility to flee. Snorting with wrath, he shortly afterwards came alongside our boat, and handed me at my request the ship's papers and asked me to tow the three boats to the neighborhood of the coast.

I promised this and said some simple words to him in regard to his bad luck and concerning the grim necessity of the war—which he dismissed with an angry shrug of his shoulders. I certainly could understand the man's bad spirit.

I then went forward and torpedoed the steamer, which sank, stern foremost, with a gurgling sound into the deep.

At the same time four thousand tons of rice were lost to the English market.

We had met with success and this put us into the highest spirits. Come whatever wants to come, our voyage had not been entirely useless.

When I stepped down into the boat for a moment and passed through the narrow crew-room to my own little cabin, I saw to right and left joyful faces, and all eyes were smiling to-

OUR FIRST SUCCESS

wards me as if they wished to say: "Congratulations!" The steamer's sinking was the subject of discussion. Those who had witnessed the incident had to describe all the circumstances in smallest detail; where the torpedo had struck, how high the water-pillar had risen, and what afterwards happened to the steamer, how the people on the boat looked, and the like. Everything had to be explained.

When I went back some one said: "To-morrow it will be in the papers." These words whirled around in my head for some time. Yes, to-morrow there would be in all the German newspapers under the column: "Ships sunk" or "Sacrifices to the U-boat war," that once more we had retaliated on our most hated enemy, that his inhuman attempt to starve our people had been parried by a horrid and strong blow. And over there upon his isle our relentless enemy would receive the same kind of a newspaper notice. The only difference was that there it would cause fury instead of joy, and the dried-up old English editor would stare terrified on the telegram which he would hold in his hand, pull off his few white threads of hair, and swear as only an Englishman can swear.

Even up to the dusk of the night, we towed the sunken freighter's three boats towards the coast. We then cut loose in order to get ready to manoeuver. When darkness set in, one had to be ready for surprises. Besides, we were not very far from land and the weather was fair, so that the boats could be in no danger. As a refreshment, I had three bottles of wine brought over to

OUR FIRST SUCCESS

the captain of the ill-fated ship, and left him with best greetings to Mr. Churchill and his colleagues.

The last streak of day became paler and paler in the west. The spook-like red cloud-riders stretched themselves more and more, became indistinct, pulled themselves asunder, and at once were swept away. In their place appeared the dark demon of the night, spread itself over heaven, hid all the stars, and settled heavily over the sea.

This was just a night suitable for us. One could not see one's hand before the eye. The steel covers on the tower windows were tightly shut, so that the least ray of light could not escape. Entirely invisible we were gliding forward in the dark. Dumb and immovable, each one was sitting at his post—the lieutenant, the subordinate officer, and the commander—trying with our eyes to pierce through the darkness and turning our heads continually from right to left and back again. The aim of our voyage was still far off and the fine weather had to be used.

Weakly, as if from a far distance, the phonograph's song reached us lonely watchmen:

"Reach me thy hand, thy dear hand;
Live well, my treasure, live well!
'Cause we travel now to Eng-eland,
Live well, my treasure, live well,
'Cause we travel now to Eng-eland."

II

AN EVENTFUL NIGHT

WHAT peculiar sensations filled me. We were at war—the most insane war ever fought! And now I am a commander on a U-boat!

I said to myself:

"You submarine, you undersea boat, you faithful U-202, which has obediently and faithfully carried me thousands of miles and will still carry me many thousand miles! I am a commander of a submarine which scatters death and destruction in the ranks of the enemy, which carries death and hell fire in its bosom, and which rushes through the water like a thoroughbred.

THE ADVENTURES OF THE U-202

What am I searching for in the cold, dark night? Do I think about honor and success? Why does my eye stare so steadily into the dark? Am I thinking about death and the innumerable mines which are floating away off there in the dark, am I thinking about enemy scouts which are seeking me?

"No! It is nerves and foolish sentiments born of foolish spirits. I am not thinking about that. Leave me alone and don't bother me. I am the master. It is the duty of my nerves to obey. Can you hear the melodious song from below, you weakling nerves? Are you so dull and faint hearted that it does not echo within you? Do you not know the stimulating power which the thin metal voice below can inspire within you?

"This song brings greetings to you

AN EVENTFUL NIGHT

from a distance of twelve hundred miles and through twelve hundred miles it comes to you. Ahead we must look; we must force our eyes to pierce the darkness on all sides."

The spy-glass flew to the eye. There is a flash in the west. A light!

"Hey, there! Hey! There is something over there——"

"That is no ordinary light. What about it?"

Lieutenant Petersen was looking through his night glasses at the light.

"I believe he is signaling," he said excitedly. "The light flashes continually to and fro. I hope it is not a scout ship trying to speak with some one."

Hardly had the lieutenant uttered these words when we all three jumped as if electrified, because certainly in our immediate neighborhood flashed before us several quick lights giving signals, which undoubtedly came from the ship second in line, which was signaling to our first friend.

"Great God! An enemy ship! Not more than three hundred meters ahead!" I exclaimed to myself.

"Hard a starboard! Both engines at highest speed ahead! To the diving stations!"

In a subdued voice, I called my commands down the tower.

The phonograph in the crew-room stopped abruptly. A hasty, eager running was discernible through the entire boat as each one hurried to his post.

The boat immediately obeyed the rudder and was flying to starboard. Between the two hostile ships there was a continuous exchange of signals.

"God be praised it is so dark!" I ex-

AN EVENTFUL NIGHT

claimed with a deep breath as soon as the first danger had passed.

"And to think that the fellow had to betray his presence by his chattering signals just as we were about to run right into his arms," was the answer. "This time we can truly say that the good God, Himself, had charge of the rudder."

The engineer appeared on the stairway which leads from the "Centrale" up to the conning tower.

"May I go to the engine-room, Herr Captain-Lieutenant?"

It was not permissible for him to leave his diving station, the "Centrale," which is situated in the center of the boat, without special permission.

"Yes, Herr Engineer, go ahead down and fire up hard!" I replied.

The thumping of the heavy oil-motors became stronger, swelled higher and higher, and, at last, became a long drawn out roar, and entirely drowned the sound of the occasional jolts which always were distinctly discernible when going at slower speed. One truly felt how the boat exerted its strength to the utmost and did everything within its power.

We had put ourselves on another course which put the anxiously signaling Britishers obliquely aport of our stern, and rushed with the highest speed for about ten minutes until their lights became smaller and weaker. We then turned point by point into our former course, and thus slipped by in a large half circle around the hostile ships.

"Just as a cat around a bowl of hot oatmeal," said Lieutenant Petersen.

"No, my dear friend," I said laugh-

AN EVENTFUL NIGHT

ingly, "it does not entirely coincide. The cat always comes back, but the oatmeal is too hot for us in this case. Or do you think that I intend to circle around those two rascals for hours?"

"Preferably not, Herr Captain-Lieutenant. It could end badly!"

"Both engines in highest speed forward, let the crew leave the diving stations, place the guards!" I ordered.

The danger had passed. Normal conditions at night could again be resumed. But before the morning set in, we again experienced all kinds of adventures. The night was as if bewitched. There was no sleep worth mentioning. I had hardly, towards ten o'clock, reached my comfortable little nest where the sailor Schultes, our own considerate "cup-bearer," had spread on my miniature writing-desk the most tempting delicacies of preserves and fruit together with a bottle of claret, when a whistle sounded in the speaking-tube on the wall right close to my head:

"Whee-e!" it shrieked, high, penetrating and alarming.

I jumped up, pulled out the stopper and put in the mouth-piece.

"Hello!"

"Two points from starboard a white light!"

I grabbed my cap and gloves and rushed sternward through the deck officer's room, petty officer's room, and crew-room, each one narrower than the other.

"Look out, the commander!" they shouted to one another, and pulled in their legs so that I could get by.

"Ouch!" I bumped my head hard against the stand of an electric lamp. I

AN EVENTFUL NIGHT

rubbed the sore spot as I hurried ahead, while I took an oath to myself that the lamp should be moved at the first possible opportunity. I hurried through the "Centrale," up the narrow stairway. Then I reached my place.

"Where?"

"There!" Lieutenant Gröning, who was on guard, pointed out. "About three points starboard!"

"It is a steamer. One can already see the red side lantern. It is crossing our course."

I put my binoculars to the eye and looked for many seconds for the light. The officer on guard was right. Besides the white lantern, one could see a deep, red light. The ship therefore was traveling towards the left and would cross our course.

A narrow strip of the moon had appeared from out of the sea and was wrestling with the darkness of the night. The result was not much—the strip of the moon was too small for that—still it was not so dark as before.

"Don't let it come too close to us!" I ordered. "And get clear in right time. We must not under any circumstances be seen by it, because then they would soon know in England from which direction to expect us. Now nearly every steamer has a wireless."

Gröning changed the course to port until he had the steamer completely to the left.

"Too bad, we can't take it with us," he said.

"No, you know, for a night attack this is not the right place. Here so many neutral steamers travel, and an error can easily be made."

AN EVENTFUL NIGHT

It was shortly after ten o'clock. At eleven-twenty, twelve forty, one-ten, three-fifteen, and five o'clock I again heard the whistling "Whee-e!" in the speaking-tube by my bunk. Each time I had to jump out of some dream, realize within a fraction of a second that my presence was desired up-stairs, grab my cap and gloves, and rush through the boat's long body up to the tower, not without several times bumping into the aforementioned and often damned electric lamp.

After five o'clock in the morning I remained on deck, because dawn would soon break with its treacherous light. The commander's post is in the tower at such a time because, just as easily as one perceives in the pale gray light a ship, one is also visible from the steamer, which could cause many unpleasant surprises if the two ships are not very cordial towards each other—especially disagreeable to us because a submarine is, as our name indicates, below the water, and the smallest fragment of a shell can badly damage our heel of Achilles, the diving machinery, so that we would be unable again to get into a position of safety beneath the surface.

Shortly before six o'clock I had the entire crew at the diving stations. Each took his place, ready at a given command to open or shut the valve, crank, or bolt of which he had charge. Only the cook had no special duty besides his own. He remained with the electric cooking apparatus provided in the galley and had no other job besides taking care of our bodily comfort. Now he was, in conformity with his duty, busy

AN EVENTFUL NIGHT

making coffee as was proper at that time of day.

A fine, strong smell of coffee percolated through the whole ship, which proved to be a great stimulant to our taut nerves and our empty stomachs.

I have to deviate a little from the subject for the purpose of asking if my readers understand me. Is it above all plain, explicit, and clear why I give so much space to a discussion of the nerves when I speak about us, U-boat men, and so often refer to them? The nerves are in time of peace the Alpha and Omega for a U-boat officer. How much more so when we are at war! The nerves to us mean power to act, decision, strength, will, and perseverance. The nerves are valuable and to keep them in good condition is of the greatest importance and an obligation and duty during a voyage.

There we sit hour after hour in the conning tower. Beneath is the most complicated mechanism the genius of man has ever created. And all around there are the most craftily constructed instruments for the purpose of destroying that which cost so much labor to create. Mines, nets, explosives, shells, and sharp keels are our enemies, which, at any moment, may send us high in the air or hundreds of meters into the ocean. Everywhere perils lurk. The whole sea is a powder barrel.

For all this there is only one remedy—nerves!

To make the right decision at the right moment is the first and last of U-boat science. One glance must be enough to determine the position. In

AN EVENTFUL NIGHT

the same second a decision must be made, and the commands carried out. A moment's hesitation may be fatal.

I can give an example of this on the very morning I speak of.

It was three minutes after six o'clock, and within about half an hour the sun would rise, but the sea and the sky still floated together in the colorless drab of early dawn and permitted one only to imagine, not see, that partition wall, the horizon.

Unceasingly our binoculars pierced the gray dusk of daybreak. Suddenly a shiver went through my body when—only a second immovable and in intense suspense—a dark shadow within range of the spy-glass made me jump. The shadow grew and became larger, like a giant on the horizon—one mast; one, two, three, four funnels—a destroyer.

A quick command—I leap down into the tower. The water rushes into the diving tanks. The conning tower covers slam tight behind me—and the agony which follows tries our patience, while we count seconds with watches in hand until the tanks are filled, and the boat slips below the sea.

Never in my life did a second seem so long to me. The destroyer, which is not more than two thousand meters distant from us, has, of course, seen us, and is speeding for us as fast as her forty thousand horse power can drive her. From the guns mounted on her bow flash one shot after another aimed to destroy us.

Good God! If he only does not hit! Just one little hit, and we are lost! Already the water splashes on the outside of the conning tower up to the glass

AN EVENTFUL NIGHT

windows through which I see the dark ghost, streaking straight for us. It is terrifying to hear the shells bursting all around us in the water. It sounds like a triphammer against a steel plate, and closer and closer come the metallic crashes. The rascal is getting our range.

There—the fifth shot—the entire boat trembles—then the deceitful daylight disappears from the conning tower window. The boat obeys the diving rudder and submerges into the sea.

A reddish-yellow light shines all around us; the indicator of the manometer, which measures our depth, points to eight meters, nine meters, ten meters, twelve meters. Saved!

What a happy, unexplainable sensation to know that you are hiding deep in the infinite ocean! The heart, which had stopped beating during these long seconds because it had no time to beat, again begins its pounding.

Our boat sinks deeper and deeper. It obeys, as does a faithful horse the slightest pressure of a rider's knees, which, in this case, are the diving rudders placed in the bow and the stern. The manometer now shows twenty-four meters, twenty-six meters. I had given orders we should go down to thirty meters.

Above us we still hear the roaring and crackling in the water, as if it were in an impotent rage. I turn and smile at the mate who is standing with me in the conning tower—a happy, care-free smile. I point upwards with my thumb.

"Do you hear it? Do you hear it?"

It is an unnecessary question, of course, because he hears it as plainly as

AN EVENTFUL NIGHT

I do, and all the others aboard hear it, too. But the question can still be explained because of the tremendous strain on our nerves which has to express itself even in such a simple question.

Dear, true, splendid little boat, how one learns to love you during such trying moments and would like to pet you like a living human being for your understanding and obedience! We, here on board, all depend upon you, just as we all depend upon one another. We are chained together. We will face the dangers together and gain success.

You blond heroes who are standing down there in the bowels of the boat without knowing what is happening up in the light, but still knowing that the crucial moment has arrived—that life or death to every one depends on one man's will and one man's decision; you who, with a calm and strong feeling of duty, stick at your posts with all the strength of your bodies and souls strained to the breaking point and still keep full faith in him who is your leader, chief, and commander; you show the highest degree of bravery and self-control, you who never have a chance to see the enemy but still, with sustained calm, do your duty.

Not a word was uttered, not a sound disturbed that deadly stillness on board. One almost forgot that the men were standing with strained nerves at their posts in order to keep the wonderful mechanism running right. One could hear the soft whirr of the dynamos and, more and more distant, the crackling of the exploding shells. Suddenly even this stopped. The Britisher must have noticed that the fish had slipped out of

AN EVENTFUL NIGHT

his hand. Shortly thereafter we heard his propellers churning the water above us. Soon this noise died away as it had come, growing fainter and fainter in a kind of grinding whirr.

"Did you hear how he circled around over us?" I asked through the speaking tube which led down into the "Centrale."

"Certainly. That could clearly be distinguished," was the short answer.

I was pondering over what to do next. At first we had no choice but to dive at the first sight of the destroyer suddenly appearing with the break of day.

In our capacity as an undersea boat, we were now in a position to fight on equal terms, and I decided to risk a bout with him as soon as it became light enough for me to see through the periscope. The intervening time I made use of by having passed up to me in the tower the long desired cup of morning coffee, in order to stop the tantalizing agony which the smell of the coffee had caused my empty stomach. Thereupon we slowly climbed upwards from our safe breakfast depth of thirty meters. The higher we came—one can read on the manometer how we are ascending meter by meter—the greater became the excitement and tension. Without breathing we listened.

Slowly the boat rose. The top of the periscope would soon be thrust above the surface. My hands clasped the handle with which the well-oiled, and therefore easily movable, periscope can be turned around as quickly as lightning, in order to take a sweep around the horizon. My eye was pressed to the

AN EVENTFUL NIGHT

sight, and soon I perceived that the water was getting clearer and clearer by degrees and more transparent. I could now follow the ascent of the boat without consulting the manometer.

My heart was pounding with the huntsman's fervor, in expectation of what I was to see at my first quick glance around the horizon, because the destroyer, which we sighted only a quarter of an hour before, could be only a scouting ship. It might belong to a detachment of naval scouts to protect a larger ship. In my thoughts I saw the whole eastern horizon full of proud ships under England's flag surrounded by smoke.

I did not see anything, no matter how carefully I scanned the horizon. All I could see was the reddening morning blush spread over half of the eastern sky, the last stars now paling and the rising sun showing its first beams.

"For heaven's sake, nobody is here," I grumbled to myself.

"Oh, he'll surely come back, Captain," said my mate with true optimism. "The prey was too hot for him to tackle and now he has started to fetch a couple more to help him."

"It would certainly be less desirable," put in Lieutenant Gröning, who, full of expectations, was standing halfway up the stairway leading from the tower to the "Centrale" and had overheard our talk. "No, it would be less desirable," he repeated, "because then comes the entire swarm of hostile U-boats with their nets cunningly lined with mines. No good will ever come of that."

"There you are right, Gröning," I agreed. "With that sort of a nuisance,

AN EVENTFUL NIGHT

equipped as they are with so many machines for our destruction, it would be very disagreeable to make their acquaintance. If they come, it is best to disappear. It is not worth the risk. We have many more important duties ahead of us. It would be too bad to spoil a good torpedo on such trash."

At the same time, I decided to rise so as to get a better observation through the periscope and once more look around the horizon. I suddenly observed in the northeast a peculiar, dark cloud of smoke. I, therefore, did not give any orders to arise, but told "Centrale" by a few short commands through the speaking tube the new turn of affairs and, with added speed, went to meet the smoke cloud.

III

THE SINKING OF THE TRANSPORT

SOON the outlines of a ship told us that ahead of us was a large steamer, steaming westward at high speed. The disappointment which we experienced at first was soon reversed when it was clearly shown that the fortunes of war had again sent a ship across our course which belonged to a hostile power.

No flag could be seen—nor was it run up. Otherwise we would have seen it.

"This is a suspicious circumstance," I reasoned with myself.

THE SINKING OF THE TRANSPORT

I called down to the "Centrale" all my observations through the periscope at regular intervals, snapping them out in the same sharp, brief style that the newsboys use in calling out the headlines to the listening public. My words were passed in whispers from mouth to mouth until all hands on board knew what was going on above the surface. Each new announcement from the conning tower caused great excitement among the crew, listening and holding their breath and, I believe, if you could measure the tension on human nerves with a barometer, it would have registered to the end of the tube, when, like hammer beats, these words went down to the "Centrale":

"The steamer's armed! Take a look, mate."

I stepped away from the sights of the

periscope. "Can you see the gun mounted forward of the bridge?"

"Yes, certainly," he replied excitedly. "I can see it, and quite a large piece it is, too."

"Now take a look at her stern—right by the second mast—what do you notice there?"

"Thousand devils! Another cannon —at least a ten-centimeter gun. It's a transport, sure."

"Drop the periscope! Port ten!" I commanded.

"Torpedo tube ready!" reported the torpedo master through the tube from the forward torpedo compartment.

By this time I had the periscope submerged so that we were completely below the surface and out of sight, and it would be impossible to discover us from

THE SINKING OF THE TRANSPORT

the steamer, even after the most careful searching of the horizon.

"Advance on the enemy!" was our determination.

Oh, what a glorious sensation is a U-boat attack! What a great understanding and coöperation between a U-boat and its crew—between dead matter and living beings! What a merging into a single being, of the nerves and spirits of an entire crew!

"Just as if the whole boat is as one being," was the thought that passed through my mind when I, with periscope down, went at my antagonist, just like a great crouching cat with her back bowed and her hair on end, ready to spring. The eye is the periscope, the brain the conning tower, the heart the "Centrale," the legs the engines, and the teeth and claws the torpedoes.

Noiselessly we slipped closer and closer in our exciting chase. The main thing was that our periscope should not be observed, or the steamer might change her course at the last moment and escape us. Very cautiously, I stuck just the tip of the periscope above the surface at intervals of a few minutes, took the position of the steamer in a second and, like a flash, pulled it down again. That second was sufficient for me to see what I wanted to see. The steamer was to starboard and was heading at a good speed across our bows. To judge from the foaming waves which were cut off from the bow, I calculated that her speed must be about sixteen knots.

The hunter knows how important it is to have a knowledge of the speed at which his prey is moving. He can cal-

THE SINKING OF THE TRANSPORT

culate the speed a little closer when it is a wounded hare than when it is one which in flight rushes past at high speed.

It was only necessary for me, therefore, to calculate the speed of the ship for which a sailor has an experienced eye. I then plotted the exact angle we needed. I measured this by a scale which had been placed above the sights of the periscope. Now I only had to let the steamer come along until it had reached the zero point on the periscope and fire the torpedo, which then must strike its mark.

You see, it is very plain; I estimate the speed of the boat, aim with the periscope and fire at the right moment.

He who wishes to know about this or anything else in this connection should join the navy, or if he is not able to do so, send us his son or brother or nephew.

On the occasion in question everything went as calculated. The steamer could not see our cautious and hardly-shown periscope and continued unconcerned on its course. The diving rudder in the "Centrale" worked well and greatly facilitated my unobserved approach. I could clearly distinguish the various objects on board, and saw the giant steamer at a very short distance —how the captain was walking back and forth on the bridge with a short pipe in his mouth, how the crew was scrubbing the forward deck. I saw with amazement—a shiver went through me —a long line of compartments of wood spread over the entire deck, out of which were sticking black and brown horse heads and necks.

THE SINKING OF THE TRANSPORT

Oh, great Scott! Horses! What a pity! Splendid animals!

"What has that to do with it?" I continually thought. War is war. And every horse less on the western front is to lessen England's defense. I have to admit, however, that the thought which had to come was disgusting, and I wish to make the story about it short.

Only a few degrees were lacking for the desired angle, and soon the steamer would get into the correct focus. It was passing us at the right distance, a few hundred meters.

"Torpedo ready!" I called down into the "Centrale."

It was the longed-for command. Every one on board held his breath. Now the steamer's bow cut the line in the periscope—now the deck, the bridge, the foremast—the funnel.

"Let go!"

A light trembling shook the boat—the torpedo was on its way. Woe, when it was let loose!

There it was speeding, the murderous projectile, with an insane speed straight at its prey. I could accurately follow its path by the light wake it left in the water.

"Twenty seconds," counted the mate whose duty it was, with watch in hand, to calculate the exact time elapsed after the torpedo was fired until it exploded.

"Twenty-two seconds!"

Now it must happen—the terrible thing!

I saw the ship's people on the bridge had discovered the wake which the torpedo was leaving, a slender stripe. How they pointed with their fingers out across the sea in terror; how the cap-

THE SINKING OF THE TRANSPORT

tain, covering his face with his hands, resigned himself to what must come. And next there was a terrific shaking so that all aboard the steamer were tossed about and then, like a volcano, arose, majestic but fearful in its beauty, a two-hundred meter high and fifty-meter wide pillar of water toward the sky.

"A full hit behind the second funnel!" I called down into the "Centrale." Then they cut loose down there for joy. They were carried away by ecstasy which welled out of their hearts, a joyous storm that ran through our entire boat and up to me.

And over there?

Landlubber, steel thy heart!

A terrible drama was being enacted on the hard-hit sinking ship. It listed and sank towards us.

THE ADVENTURES OF THE U-202

From the tower I could observe all the decks. From all the hatches human beings forced their way out, fighting despairingly. Russian firemen, officers, sailors, soldiers, hostlers, the kitchen crew, all were running and calling for the boats. Panic stricken, they thronged about one another down the stairways, fighting for the life-boats, and among all were the rearing, snorting and kicking horses. The boats on the starboard deck could not be put into service, as they could not be swung clear because of the list of the careening steamer. All, therefore, thronged to the boats on the port side, which, in the haste and anguish, were lowered, some half empty; others overcrowded. Those who were left aboard were wringing their hands in despair. They ran from bow to stern and back again from stern to bow in

THE SINKING OF THE TRANSPORT

their terror, and then finally threw themselves into the sea in order to attempt to swim to the boats.

Then another explosion resounded, after which a hissing white wave of steam streamed out of all the ports. The hot steam set the horses crazy, and they were beside themselves with terror—I could see a splendid, dapple-gray horse with a long tail make a great leap over the ship's side and land in a lifeboat, already overcrowded—but after that I could not endure the terrible spectacle any longer. Pulling down the periscope, we submerged into the deep.

When, after some time, I came again to the surface there was nothing more to be seen of the great, proud steamer. Among the wreckage and corpses of the horses three boats were floating and occasionally fished out a man still swimming in the sea. Now I came up on the surface in order to assist the victims of the wrecked ship. When our boat's mighty, whale-like hull suddenly arose out of the water, right in their midst, a panic seized them again and quickly they grasped their oars in order to try to flee. Not until I waved from the tower to them with my handkerchief and cap did they rest on their oars and come over to us. The state in which some of them were was exceedingly pitiful. Several wore only white cotton trousers and had handkerchiefs wrapped around their necks. The fixed provisions which each boat was required to carry were not sufficient when the boat's crew was doubled and trebled.

While I was conferring with our mess officer as to what we could possibly dispense with of our own provisions we noticed to the north and west some clouds of smoke which, to judge from the signs, were coming towards us quickly. Immediately a thought flashed through my head:

"Now they are looking for you. Now comes the whole swarm."

Already the typical masts of the British destroyers and trawlers arose above the horizon. We, therefore, did not have a minute to lose in order to escape these hostile and most dangerous enemies. I made my decision quickly and called to the captain of the sunken steamer that he could let one of the oncoming ships pick them up as I could not spare the time, but had to go "northeast." Then I submerged—right in front of the boats full of survivors. They saw me head north and I steered in that direction for a time. Then I pulled down the periscope and, without being noticed, changed my course to the south.

When I, after a considerable time, again cautiously looked around, I perceived to my amazement that an entire scout fleet in a wide circle was heading towards us from the south also. From three sides the enemy spurred his bloodhounds on us, and I thought to myself it would not take long before, by extending their wings, they would encircle us completely, and the great chase would begin. The thought was not cheerful, particularly as the depths in this part of the ocean were not sufficient so that we could, by submerging deeply, guard ourselves against the dangers of grappling hooks, nets and mines.

THE SINKING OF THE TRANSPORT

"The wildcat has become a hare," I thought to myself and, at the same time, I decided what to do.

We had to do as the old hare. First, with eyes open, we would cautiously jump forth, use all possible covers, and search for the spot where the gunners were fewest, and then with eyes shut and at the highest possible speed break through the widest gap.

Consequently, we began to travel toward the east where the "atmosphere was still clear." Occasionally I stuck up my periscope and perceived how the surrounding circle was knit tighter and tighter. Now, after I had made up my mind, I became completely calm and carefully considered all the conditions for and against us. The swarm of destroyers moved toward the center, as in a regular chase, as soon as the circle was complete. Between every couple of hunters—I mean trawlers—there were nets stretched across to catch a little submarine, and behind these were dragged mines.

By extending one of the wings in the north, it made a gap toward the east, and besides I saw that one of the torpedo boats between two groups of the searching parties had left for the shipwrecked survivors. At this point, consequently, was our best chance to escape. I laid my course between the two searching parties, of course, with the periscope, during the whole time, nearly invisible.

Slowly the ranks of the hunting hounds approached, smoking copiously and snorting. Now the right moment had arrived to follow the other part of the hare's program. We shut our

THE SINKING OF THE TRANSPORT

eyes—that is, I pulled the periscope down completely—and proceeded with increased speed, submerging in the sea as deeply as possible.

I can well imagine how the old hare felt when he ran blindly for his life. Undoubtedly our feelings were somewhat the same. How easily could not that little gap toward which we were making be closed by some small auxiliary of the searchers.

And, if the grappling hooks from one of these got hold of us, there would be little hope of escape, or of saving ourselves. Then they would tear at us from all directions and give us the stab that would send us deep down into the sea for good. No one on board suspected what danger we went to meet. I had kept all my observations concerning the enemy's surrounding us to myself and had not mentioned it, so as not to excite everybody's mind. No one below could at any rate do anything to change the conditions.

Then from the bow compartment came the report:

"The beating of propellers is discernible to port!"

Shortly thereafter I could hear them, even from the conning tower—a soft, slow, swelling, and grinding sound. This was not the sound of the propellers of a destroyer. Such would beat faster, clearer, and more powerfully. This was the heavily-dragging trawlers' slow beating propellers.

Strainingly I listened to starboard—nothing could be heard. That was a good sign, because I could hope that in reality I had reached the gap and that the sounds of the propellers which we

THE SINKING OF THE TRANSPORT

heard to port emanated from the trawler on the left side of the gap. I was just about, from my innermost heart, to let out a joyous "hurrah," when, from the bow of the boat, I heard a new sound which approached with a clear, sharp banging. It was the torpedo-boat, the beast! Was the rascal going to come back at the crucial moment?

It required only a few seconds for the torpedo-boat to pass over us, but those seemed as hours. At every blinking of the eye I imagined I heard something explode, turn against or drag alongside my boat. But fortune was ours. The sharp, grinding sound of the swift torpedo-boat propellers became fainter and fainter and, at last, ceased entirely. Unconsciously I straightened up a little in the tower, whistled a few notes from "Dockan," and tapped, as if nothing had happened, with the knuckle of my forefinger on the glass of the manometer. What did the manometer register? Nothing whatsoever had happened. Everything was in the best condition. The depth coincided. The diving rudder was lying normal. Before me stood Tuczynski, my faithful helmsman and orderly, at former times skipper on the *Weichsel* and *Nogat;* behind me, the mate leaned against the wall of the conning tower contentedly and yawned.

I suddenly felt an unresistible craving for a cigarette. The nerves needed some stimulation. For about ten minutes I controlled myself. Then I arose to a periscope distance from the surface and took a look around to see how things were going. What I saw filled

THE SINKING OF THE TRANSPORT

my heart with joy. The whole swarm of British destroyers and trawlers had moved toward the southwest and were eagerly searching in a long line. As we were proceeding in an opposite direction we quickly left them. After about five more minutes I would dare to come to the surface. To the north the way was clear.

Soon I was sitting, in the best of spirits, up in the conning tower, greedily inhaling with both lungs the fine, refreshing sea air and, mixed with it, the long puffs of the cigarette.

IV

RICH SPOILS

LATE in the afternoon of the same day we broke into a peacefully working fishing flotilla just like a wolf into a flock of sheep. In order to be sure no shepherd with his dog was guarding them we, keeping ourselves submerged, carefully examined each ship. I could not see a gun or anything suspicious anywhere.

All were peacefully occupied at their casting nets, fishing. There were seven fishing steamers and nine sailing ships, which were scattered over a distance of about three miles. The weather was

RICH SPOILS

glorious, even better than the day before. The sun smiled from a steel blue sky and danced in golden stripes on the bright, calm surface of the sea. A gentle northerly swell rocked the fishing boats back and forth, so that the gaffs and the frames on which the extra nets had been stretched to dry were swinging and banging.

Countless numbers of sea gulls were flying about close to the flotilla. With shrill cries and in thick flocks, they swooped down on the sterns of some isolated boats, and hurled themselves, gliding on their wings, into the refuse of the last catch which the fishermen were throwing overboard.

The horizon stood out visibly from the sea all around and seemed to be a great shining, glittering ring. Not a speck of cloud spotted its bright edges.

Nothing was visible except our fishermen.

Hurrah, this was just the weather for us! A rare and favorable opportunity had presented itself here to play a trick on the English fish market.

As a ghost, I suddenly arose behind one of the fishing steamers, pushed the conning tower hatch up, and jumped up on the tower, holding the flag of war in one hand and the megaphone in the other.

"Halloo-o-o!"

The fishermen stared at us open mouthed, rooted to the spot as if paralyzed by fear of us.

"Halloo-o-o-o, Captain!" I shouted for the second time. "I want to talk to you."

After some time a figure emerged from the crowd, stepped up the stairway, and shouted some words that were not very clear but which sounded like:

"Here I am!"

I summoned my best English and told the red-nosed chap that I would have to sink before sundown the whole fleet of fishing boats, and furthermore I told him that I had selected him to take the crews of all the others aboard his steamer. I added he must immediately cut his nets and follow me at a distance of five hundred meters, and that I would promptly blow him to pieces if he, of his own accord, attempted to diminish this distance as I would then surely believe he intended to ram me.

The captain declared he was willing to obey my commands, cut the nets, and followed me. I ordered full speed ahead and hoisted to the mast the following signal:

"Leave the boat immediately!"

Then I rushed in among the excited swarm. With flashing eyes, the sailors were standing by our guns and waiting, lovingly fondling the shells, ready to begin firing.

First we went right through the crowd of fishing-boats and then along the edges of the fleet, in order to prevent the escape of the steamers furthest away. Nowhere did we take the time to stop to sink a ship, but only drove the crews away from their boats. Then the prey could not get away from us.

How promptly the fishermen alighted because of the fear of our shells! They scrambled aboard the one steamer selected to save them in such a rush it

RICH SPOILS

looked like a panicky flight. Soon cutters and rowboats were swarming all around us and speedily the steamer selected to save the crews was crowded.

But even during such an exciting occupation we did not neglect to keep a sharp lookout, for under no circumstances were we to be taken by surprise when at this work. But it was easy to look out over a great distance. The horizon was free and clear.

As soon as the fishermen were safe aboard the steamer, we began the sinking of the ships and went from ship to ship, stopped at a distance of a hundred meters, and sent solid, well-aimed shots at their water lines until they had had enough and began to sink. Many went down with the first shot. Others were tougher and required four. For the gun crew this was great sport. They took turns and each jealously counted the number of shots required for his "fisherman."

When the steamers were "fixed," we went to the sailing boats, which, in accordance with their inveterate custom, were lying huddled together. The sailors generally needed only one shot —then they capsized and sank into the sea with a death gurgle. It was a touching scene which, in spite of our inner joy, was hard on our nerves, as every true sailor regards the sailing-ship as a remnant of romance, dying out faster and faster in these days.

This was truly the reason why now and at other times our hearts ached for each sailing ship which we had to sink. The surface was covered with hundreds of thousands of dead fish which were scattered over the sea. To countless sea

RICH SPOILS

gulls it was a highly welcome call to dinner, which they eagerly accepted, gorging themselves and filling themselves so that their feathers stood straight out from their bodies.

We had already sent thirteen ships to the bottom, only two sailing-ships remaining besides the rescue steamer. As the opportunity was a rare one, I permitted the firemen and men from the engine room to come up on deck so that they could see with their own eyes a ship go down. I enjoyed hearing their funny remarks and to watch how, in their childish joy, they enthusiastically greeted each new shot. I was glad to see the bright color the fresh air and excitement brought to their pale faces. Gröning stepped up to me and said thoughtfully:

"What will happen if the steamer

goes to England and tells our position? Following the events of yesterday afternoon, this morning and now, the English can easily figure out our course."

"By Jove, you are right there! I had not happened to think of that. It is indeed true that one gets duller as the years go by. That must be prevented under all circumstances, especially on account of to-morrow. You know what then—don't you?"

Gröning nodded.

"Yes, to-morrow we'll have a trying day," I continued, "and, if we are going to succeed, we can't make conditions any harder for ourselves."

I was pondering the question of how we were going to avoid the danger of being betrayed by the fishermen without endangering their lives, which I did not want to do. I thought this over for a

RICH SPOILS

moment. Suddenly I struck my forehead with my hand and laughed.

"So stupidly foolish! One is never able to think of the simplest way!" I said. "We'll simply shift the entire crowd to one of the sailing-ships. With this light breeze, it will take them at least three days to reach the coast and, after that, it does not matter. It will be a little crowded for so many people, but that can't be helped."

"And the provisions?" Gröning asked. "What are they going to live on?"

"That's simple," I answered. "First of all they can take off all the provisions from the steamer and, besides that, they have all the fish in the sailing-ship."

I sank the smaller of the two sailboats and then approached the steamer which had taken aboard the crews from the other boats.

The captain of the steamer was bitterly disappointed, of course, when I brought him word that all hands would have to go to the sailboat. He had been so delighted to be the one chosen to keep his steamer. On the other hand, to the captain of the sailing-ship, the message that he could go back to his old, faithful smack came as a gift from heaven.

Yes, indeed, joy and sorrow lie close together and go hand in hand.

After a short half hour the shift was made, and the steamer also went down into the deep—the fifteenth ship within two hours. First the skipper carefully hauled up his nets and then with flapping sails slowly swung around and laid his course toward the west.

During the night we dropped down

to the bottom of the ocean at X——. We wanted to get some rest for one night and gather strength for the next day. It is comfortable to lie in the soft sands of the North Sea. It is as if the whole boat went to bed. One thing necessary for this comfort was a calm surface, because a heavy sea is felt at a great depth and throws and bangs the boat back and forth on the bottom.

Slowly the boat slipped deeper and deeper. We had taken soundings before submerging. The nearer we came to the bottom the slower the dynamo motors worked, and I at last stopped them entirely when we were a few meters from the bottom. As soon as we had stopped sinking, which could be told by the fact the diving rudder was no longer working, a few liters of water were pumped into a ballast tank made for just this purpose. The boat became heavier and slowly sunk further.

"Now, we'll soon strike," I called down to the "Centrale" and looked at the manometer.

Hardly had the words left my lips when we felt a very gentle shock—much weaker than when a train stops—and knew we were at the bottom. Some more water was pumped into the ballast tanks in order to make the boat steadier and then each one at his post carefully examined scuttles and hatchways so that not a drop of water could leak through to us. From bow to stern it was reported:

"All is tight!"

Thereafter orders were given for the necessary guards, and then I let the crew leave their posts:

"All hands to be free to-night!"

RICH SPOILS

Until to-morrow on the bottom of the ocean! No other restfulness can be compared with it. Rest after so much excitement which has stirred the emotions of us all; after such a day's work, is it possible that any one can appreciate how we enjoyed ourselves?

We did not care that we were not in port and that a mountain of ocean was over our heads. We felt as secure as if we had been at the safest spot in the world. From their posts the crew went past us, with pale, oily, and dirty faces, but with their eyes looking at me as they went by, proud, happy, radiant, so that my heart rejoiced.

There was some excitement among the crew. Every one washed, talked and laughed so that it was evident how happy and care-free they felt.

"Well, with what will you treat us

to-day?" I asked the cook who, with great self-confidence—because he was an expert in his line—was standing before his little galley and stirring a steaming pot. "That smells wonderfully appetizing."

"Ox goulash and salt potatoes," answered the cook and with more eagerness stirred his pot. "It soon will be ready. It'll not take more than five minutes."

"Then I must hurry up," I replied, and went to my small cabin, where I had not put foot since five o'clock in the morning.

I put my cap, long scarf and oil-skin jacket on a hook, stretched myself in weary delight and washed myself energetically. This is a rare pleasure on a trip like ours. From the nearby room the happy talk of the officers reached

RICH SPOILS

my ears. I then heard a rattle of plates and forks, a cork popped from a bottle, and Gröning opened the little door that separates my cabin from the room of the other officers.

"Herr Captain, dinner is ready," he said.

Soon we were sitting, four men in all, at a little, nicely decorated table, cutting into the steaming platter and drinking out of small seidels a magnificent sparkling wine. The past day's events had to be moistened a little with the best we had. This was our custom when the fortunes of war smiled graciously on us.

The electrical heating apparatus furnishes all the heat needed, but it still has the disadvantage that in the still, unchanged air, the heat arises so that the temperature at the floor is several degrees colder than at the ceiling. Even in our heavy sea-boots, we felt it a little, although, as a whole, we were warm and contented. The phonograph played continuously. The petty officers had taken charge of it and played one native song after another. What a thrill ran through me! At once there was silence. All talk stopped. German songs of the Fatherland were sung deep down at the bottom of the ocean right on England's coast. Inspired by the music, our hearts were filled with enthusiasm and a silent promise was made to give everything for the Fatherland—to become a scourge to the enemy and damage him with all our might.

Thereafter, the dance music, operettas, vaudeville songs, and ragtime were played. These stirred up a buoyant spirit. Especially there was much

RICH SPOILS

joy among the firemen and sailors in the crew's quarters. Funny songs could be heard from that direction. Dirty playing cards were dug out and soon there was a real German skat game in full swing.

During this time we, in the officers' mess, raised our glasses and drank toasts to one another and to the beautiful U-boat: "Rich spoils! A happy journey home! Long live the U-boat!" That is the U-boat toast.

The boat was lying very still. It didn't seem to stir.

"What an original idea for an artist!" said our engineer, who was poetically inclined, as he leaned back in his chair staring thoughtfully at the ceiling. "One can imagine a cross section of the boat showing our room at the North Sea's yellowish sand bottom, to which all kinds of crawling and swimming animals give life. In here four feasting, happy officers around a little table on which a warm electric light is shining with the wine bottle in the center and with the glasses raised to a solemn toast. Above—water, water, water—water to the height of a church steeple and, over it all, the glittering heavens full of stars and a small silver-white piece of the moon. If I were a painter I should immediately start with this motive for a picture."

"And give me the picture, I hope," I laughed. "And, after all, not such a bad idea about that picture—one should in reality propose such a motive to an artist."

"Maybe it would be possible to put in a couple of mermaids who look in through the conning tower window inquisitively and knock with their fingers on the glass," said Petersen, our youngest lieutenant, with a smile. "That would undoubtedly make the picture still more attractive."

Gröning, who during the entire time had listened with a quiet smile to the conversation, took out his empty cigar holder, on which he always chewed when we were under water because, as a heavy smoker, he missed tobacco, as none of us was allowed to smoke inside the boat. Slowly he said with a touch of irony, in a deep, sympathetic voice:

"Here, my dear Petersen, you are an unreasonable rascal. If there are no women in the game, then there is no pleasure for you. Doesn't the fellow actually talk about mermaids when he tells us every fourth week he is going to become engaged. 'This time it's absolutely certain! This time I surely will do it, as I will never find such a girl again.' This and more I hear every month. What was the last one's name that you intended to make happy—your March girl? Wait, I have it—the February girl—ha, ha, ha—has the captain heard the story of the February girl?"

He turned to me laughing.

"Will you shut up, Gröning!" Petersen burst forth and blushed up to his ears. "I'll tell you that if you tell tales out of school—and besides——"

"Well, Petersen," I encouraged, "what 'besides'?"

"Besides, all that is not true," he continued and blushed still more when he noticed that he had betrayed himself. "*You* should certainly keep quiet," he went on suddenly, beaming with an idea, and began to attack in order to lead the conversation away from himself. "He who lives in glass houses should be more careful."

"I-I-I—how so—that's the limit!" Gröning angrily rejoined, as he considered it an honor to be known among his friends as a woman hater. "I—in a glass house? It's a mean accusation, or have you been drinking too much wine, my dear boy?"

"Bah! only a glass," answered the younger officer, defending himself. "It is ridiculous to claim anything like that."

"Well, well, be friends now, sirs," I said soothingly. "Don't let's quarrel down here at the bottom of the sea. I hereby decide that our younger officer is absolutely sober, but that, even so, he will not be allowed to let his April girl with her fishtail come in here, as a punishment, because he has jilted his February girl."

With this decision both these fighting roosters (really the best friends in the world) had to be pleased, and the eternal discussion of Eve and her daughters, which had nearly made the ocean bottom shake under our feet, was ended.

Shortly after this we went to bed in our narrow bunks—for the first time undressed on the voyage—and soon enjoyed a sleep free from dreams.

V

THE WITCH-KETTLE

IN the morning no rooster crowed to wake me. But, instead, there stood my faithful orderly, the Pole, Tuczynski, before my bed, and loudly announced:

"Herr Captain Lieutenant, it's five-thirty!"

I woke up in bewilderment. My head was still dull after a sound sleep.

"What's up?"

"It's five-thirty," repeated the orderly. "The water for washing and the clothes are ready."

Ah! Like a flash the reality was before me. We were lying on the bottom of the sea—were going to arise within an hour—and then we were going to——

I leaped out of bed. The thought of "then we were going to" fully awoke me. "Yes, we are going to go at it; everything depends upon to-day," I thought, and put my feet into my slippers.

Hardly had I scrambled to my feet when I had to grasp the closet to support myself.

"What's up now?" I asked, turning to my good Pole, who was spitting on my left boot in order to preserve the shine. "We are rolling. What's happened?"

"Must be a little sea above," he replied with a grin.

"I can understand that myself, you

THE WITCH-KETTLE

smarty, but when did it start? Run along quickly and find out when the rolling was first noticed!"

Tuczynski hurried to the "Centrale" and returned immediately with his answer:

"About two o'clock, says Lieutenant Petersen."

"Well, then we must have a considerable storm above, if the wind has been blowing for four hours. Get out my oil-skin coat quickly! It will be needed to-day," I ordered, and hurriedly dressed myself as water-tight as possible.

The change of weather did not suit my purpose, for, although to judge from the motion of the boat the storm was not as yet so bad, the strength of the wind was probably six, and it was gradually becoming worse. At this time of the year storms could be terrible.

"Devil take the luck—and this very day, too!" I swore through my six-day old beard-stub.

After breakfast I called the entire crew together. "Boys," I said, "you know that we have many things unaccomplished. As yet we are only at the beginning of our task. Yesterday and the day before we were very successful, and now we have had a restful night. Being well rested, we are now cheerfully and confidently ready for another day's work. To-day we are going to go through the so-called 'Witch-Kettle.' You all know what I mean, and you know also that this is not child's play. The enemy there is keeping sharp lookout, but we will keep a better look-out. Others have gotten through before us.

THE WITCH-KETTLE

Consequently, we will also get through, if each one of you sticks to his post and does his duty as well as you all have done hitherto. This I expect from every man. And now—to the diving stations!"

I went up to the tower. Shortly after the engineer reported from the "Centrale":

"All hands are at the diving station!"

Consequently we were ready for our task. The day began—the most remarkable day of my life.

"Arise!"

The pump began to buzz. We now had to empty the ballast-tanks of the water which had been taken in to make the boat heavier, in order that, instead of being held down, we should begin to pull ourselves loose, and drift slowly upwards. Usually that manœuver was accomplished with the best of success, but not so to-day. The boat wabbled and "stuck," as we used to say. It called to my mind the question which is often asked by laymen: "Are you never in fear of not being able to get up to the surface again?" We, of course, had no fear, but I knocked impatiently on the manometer to see if the register would not at last begin to move.

"Nine hundred liters above the normal," Krüger reported from the "Centrale."

It meant that we had pumped out of the boat nine hundred liters more than the normal quantity necessary to make the boat rise.

"It seems as if we were fastened in a vise," I joked, "but in accordance with the map there ought to be a sand bottom here."

THE WITCH-KETTLE

"Now it loosens!" the engineer called out.

Yes, the boat pulled loose all right—the hand on the manometer was rising—but it shot upwards on one side only. The stern arose but the nose remained fastened in the mud.

"How confoundedly nasty," I heard Gröning, who took care of the diving rudder, growl.

Now the entire ballast shifted. We had to make the boat heavier in the stern, had to shift the ballast of the heretofore well-balanced boat and pump ballast water out of the bow to pour water into the stern tanks, in order to make the bow lighter and the stern heavier. After a few liters of water had exchanged places the boat changed her mind and again placed herself in a horizontal position. Then she arose quickly and satisfactorily, but showed a tendency to list toward the stern, until we, by a new shift of the ballast, had reestablished the old conditions of equilibrium.

After the boat had pulled loose with apparent reluctance from her bed on the bottom, she could not get up fast enough to stick her nose into the fresh air. Having the ballast diminished by nine hundred liters, she leaped upwards rapidly, but this did not suit my purpose, as I preferred first to put up the periscope and find out whether the atmosphere was free from British germs. As I felt I was entirely responsible for my boat's health, I entertained one fear, based on experience, that germs in the form of destroyers and trawlers, appearing suddenly, might endanger it. I made the boat obey my

THE WITCH-KETTLE

will, let the nine hundred liters be pumped into her again, and thus checked her quick ascent.

At the same time I had the dynamo motors started, so that we would have steerageway for the diving rudder, and commanded that the U-boat should stop at the depth of twenty meters. Thereafter, I soon came to the periscope depth and took a look around to see if I could discover any ships. There was nothing in sight, but woe—a heavy storm!

"Well, it can't be helped," I said softly to myself.

I made another careful search of the horizon and then arose entirely to the surface. What a delightful sensation to be standing on the tower with my hands to my sides and greedily sucking my lungs full of the fresh sea air! The air at the bottom had not been so bad. On the contrary, the engineers had kept it in first-class condition during the night, but more delightful was the wonderful ocean air.

Now the ventilator burst open and refreshed those inside with fresh air throughout the ship.

"Now, Mate," I ordered, "let me take a look at the map once more. That's right. Put it right up here on the tower —no harm done if it gets wet. Now let's have a compass and a lead pencil —thanks. Watch carefully and follow my calculations to see I make no mistake. From here to the first mine field it is twenty-two miles; from there to the second mine field about fourteen miles—which makes thirty-six miles altogether. We must reach the first field just before the ebb tide, as the mines are

THE WITCH-KETTLE

only visible just before or right after the ebb tide. We get the ebb about ten o'clock, and it is now half past six. We can, therefore, go along easily at half speed and will have enough time to recharge the batteries. Is that right?"

"Yes, that's right," replied the mate, and quickly folded up the map, which he had shown anxiety in guarding, time and time again, against the waves washing over the ship, "if we only don't have to dive again."

"I don't believe we will," I said with confidence. "Here near the mine fields I think there are few ships sailing. So far as that goes, we are really safer here. The scouting will be on the other side of the fields."

Exactly one hour before the ebb tide we reached those sections where the enemy, according to the reports from other U-boats, believed that they had effectively blocked the passage with a mine field that stretched for several miles. I say "believed," because the mines, as before stated, were showing above the surface during the ebb tide and one could easily steer through the lanes between them. The blocking of this important passage was therefore for the enemy an assuring but somewhat expensive illusion. It was not quite so easy as I had expected from the stories and reports of my fellow submarine commanders to slip between the mines.

"Well, sirs, here it goes!" I said to both officers, who, like me, had crawled into their thick oil-skins and had exchanged their caps, embroidered with gold oak leaves, for the practical south-

THE WITCH-KETTLE

wester. "Now, we'll see who spots the first mine."

In a drizzle of foam and spray we were standing side by side and gazed at the sea several hundred meters ahead of us. The ocean had within the last few hours become still heavier and stormier, and the wind came from the southwest and consequently straight toward us so that there was danger of discovering the mines too late, as they would be concealed from our sight with every roll of the sea.

Suddenly we all three looked at one another and then quickly at the sea again. There they were! Heavens, what a bunch! In all directions as far as the eye could see were the devilish dark globes, washed with the breakers' snow-white foam. We were so overwhelmed by the sight of all these mines that we started to swear and kept it up for some time without any interruption.

"It's outrageous! It's unheard of! It's terrible! Such a mass! And such a people call themselves Christian seafarers—a bunch of murderers, that's what they are, who can put out such dirty traps!"

With reduced speed we went toward the "caviar sandwich," as Petersen called the dark spotted surface before us. Now it was "up to" us skilfully to steer the boat between the irregularly spread mines and see carefully to it that we did not get into a blind alley. If only our boat did not hit one of those devilish things! It would be the end of us! But surely if we kept calm, we should get through all right. Certainly we would. We had a warhelmsman who was a wonder in his line, boat-

THE WITCH-KETTLE

swain's mate Lohmann. He could thank his skill as a helmsman for his long career in the navy. If he was up to some deviltry—which, it is said, rather often happened in former days—it was always mentioned as an extenuating circumstance—"but he's such an able helmsman."

Lohmann, when he put his mind to it, could certainly steer. He could hit a floating cork with the prow. He was standing with feet apart in the tower and grinning so that his mouth reached from ear to ear. He always grinned when he stood at the wheel. But now that he had become the most important person on board, he was radiating joy and pride to such an extent that his little square figure took on a superior pose of careless daring. With his right hand he spun the wheel playfully, just as if he were experimenting. He had shoved the other deep down into the large pocket of his seaman's trousers clear up to his elbow.

Then we were pounding into the mine field. Lohmann squinted together his small gray eyes to a couple of narrow slits, spat first in his right hand, and then in a long semi-circle towards the first mine which we were just passing on the port side. He, thereupon, hitched his slipping trousers, lit his nose-warmer—a pipe broken off close to the bowl—spat once more into his right hand, and began a series of artistic curvings and twistings to weave his way through the narrow lanes. And he was as calm and confident as if he had done nothing all his life except steer U-boats through mine fields. I could leave him in charge of it.

THE WITCH-KETTLE

After ten minutes we had passed the mine field. We estimated we had sifted through about eight hundred mines.

At high speed we then steered toward the second batch of mines.

Then came a series of reverses which made this the most eventful day so far experienced by any U-boat crew in the war.

It was ten forty-two by the clock.

Beyond the second mine field an English destroyer was patrolling. We had to dive quickly and go through the mines under the water, a detested and very dangerous proceeding!

The destroyer had not seen us. The sea became more violent; the barometer fell rapidly; the heaven was filled with black rain clouds. The clearness of the atmosphere disappeared, and the ocean was restless and covered with white foam. The sea washed over the periscope again and again with white-combed, rushing mountains of water, so that for several long seconds I could see nothing. Suddenly we were in the midst of the mines. I could make out those that were close by, because the water had risen so that only the tops of the black balls, which here and there bobbed up for a second, could be seen.

To turn away from the mines at the right moment was almost impossible. We were running straight for a mine—the next second it was on top of us and passed only a few meters from the periscope. At the same time, on the other side, three mines clustered together in a group were floating past us. It was a hellish journey, and the destroyer was all the time waiting for us on the other side of the mine field, and compelled us

THE WITCH-KETTLE

to continue below the surface. He had no consideration for our difficulties.

Oh, how he would enjoy it if we suddenly went up in the air, surrounded by a cloud of smoke and fire! Good God! Now we are about to give him this joy. I had already shut my eyes and thought we were doomed—because one of the mines had just struck hard with a metallic clang against the periscope, a sound which I will never forget until I am in a better world! But the mine, which I saw just before the wave washed over the periscope, had been carried away behind us and had better sense than to blow us up; it only twisted on its axis and didn't do us any harm. Maybe it was old and damaged.

I could not stand it any longer. I felt like a man trying to commit suicide when he misses his aim.

"Quickly dive to twenty-five meters!" I called down to the "Centrale."

Rather dash blindly through this hell than always see your last minute right before your eyes, and still be unable to do anything. But if, while submerged, a cable should fasten itself around the U-boat? The chance of getting through was better down there, I figured.

"Start the phonograph," I commanded, "and put on something cheerful, if you please!"

In spite of the new, beautiful "Field Gray Uniforms," the song which soon resounded through the boat, I heard twice a hellish grinding and scraping above the conning tower—mine cables which we had fouled. At last, after many long minutes, we were through the mine field. We arose and I put up the periscope and looked around. God be praised! The atmosphere, or rather the water, was clearer. The destroyer was several hundred meters behind us, and we had come through the horrible place without a scratch.

Aha! There was the first buoy—the first placed on the narrow sand bar. Now it was careful steering for the ship. We took soundings and proceeded cautiously. If only the current had not been so strong! It constantly swung us out of our course. I had to steer against the current continually.

"Mate, how far are we now from land?"

The sailor quickly brought up the chart and measured the distance with a scale.

"Two and a half sea miles."

"Oh, the devil! And, as yet, we cannot see anything of it. The air has been thickening. That's all we need to make things worse for us!"

The cruiser on guard now came rushing past us on the port side. It was not far from us when I pulled down the periscope for a time.

Who can describe my fright when I put up the periscope again in a few minutes and could not see anything because of the fog that had settled down on the sea! A dark rainwall also moved along the surface. And this was just where it was absolutely necessary for me to see. I must see where the channel began to be very narrow! Only one narrow passage about two hundred meters wide, there was, within which we absolutely must proceed. Every turn away from this—either to the right or left—would immediately run us into the sandbank. And now there was no sign of

THE WITCH-KETTLE

the buoy which marked the channel. In addition to this we faced a current we had not counted on.

I searched and searched for the buoy. The sweat stood out on my forehead, and the excitement made me so warm that the sights on the periscope time and time again clouded up on account of the heat from my body. The mate must continually wipe the wet glass with a piece of chamois.

"Now we should be off the buoy, Mate, but I don't see it! Good God, what are we going to do! It will be fatal—it is impossible to navigate without picking it up. And besides, the destroyer which is lurking behind that confounded rainwall and which at any minute can come up alongside us!"

The buoy did not appear.

Then the weather began to clear up.

THE ADVENTURES OF THE U-202

The rain thinned and the fog lifted a little.

First we saw land. Thereafter we saw the destroyer at quite a distance on the port side, laying a course towards us, and then—then——

All good spirits have mercy on us!

The buoy—our buoy—was to the wrong side.

And we? Great God in Heaven—we were going on the wrong course! We were running right for the sand-bank. We must already be right on top of them. Disastrously for us, it has cleared too late.

"Hard a-starboard! Reverse both engines full speed!" There was nothing more to do. Then came the disaster! A jar and a whirring—U-boat 202 had gone aground.

VI

A DAY OF TERROR

WHAT we went through was horrible. The breakers dashed high over the sandbar. They hurled themselves on us to destroy our boat, played ball with us, lifted us high into the air and dropped us again on the bar with such fury that the whole boat shivered and trembled.

We had lost control of the boat completely. The roaring breakers made so much noise we could hear them through the thick metal wall. Every new, onrushing wave tossed us higher and higher on the reef. Exposure was our greatest danger. Already the top of the conning tower and the prow projected above the surface—but a moment more and the entire boat would be plainly visible. Then we would surely be lost. As a helpless wreck, we would become a target for the destroyer.

Pale and calm, every man stuck to his post and clung to the nearest support, so as not to fall at the rolling and jolting of the boat. With awe, I looked alternately at the manometer and the feverish sea which I could see all around me through the conning tower windows. Oh, if it had been only the sea we must fear! But through the scum and froth, more merciless than the wild, onrushing breakers, the black destroyer, smoking copiously, steamed straight toward us, like a bull with lowered horns.

"We had better keep below the water at any price, even if we are smashed to

A DAY OF TERROR

pieces against the sandbank and the boat breaks up, rather than to be blown to pieces by the shells of the English," was the thought that flashed through my brain.

"Fill the ballast tanks," I called down to the "Centrale." "Fill all the tanks full, Herr Engineer. Do you hear? We must not under any circumstances rise any higher!"

"All ballast tanks filling!" it was reported from below.

Oh, how quiet it was below! Not a word was uttered. No anxious conjectures, no surmises, and no questions.

A deep, irresistible grief clutched my heart. My poor little boat! My poor crew! There every man unflinchingly and unhesitatingly did his duty, and devotedly put his faith in me. They were all heroes, so young and still so brave and able. And I, the commander, had brought them into the very mouth of death, and to me, the only one who could see our desperate situation, it seemed as if the scale of death slowly weighed against us, because the destroyer, with horrible certainty, was approaching. His sharp prow pointed directly towards us. Soon he would discover the projecting parts of our tower and prow, which the breakers treacherously washed over, and then we would be lost. Soon a hail of shells would sweep over us, and the greedy, foaming sea would roaringly hurl itself through the open holes in our sides.

The filling of the ballast tanks had the desired effect. The boat lay down heavily on the reef and spurred the wild waves to greater efforts, and, though we did not rise any farther, the jolting increased in violence because of its added weight. It was a wonder that the boat did not go to pieces like an egg shell, and we all looked at one another in surprise when, after a terrific jolt, nothing more occurred than the bursting of a few electric bulbs. "First-class material," I thought to myself.

The mate who, over my shoulder, was keeping watch on the destroyer through the window on the port side, suddenly said, in his hearty, Saxon dialect:

"Well, well! Where does he intend to look for us now, I wonder? At any rate, he doesn't think that we are stuck here among the breakers."

"Mate, you old optimist. Those words I'll never forget. Great God! If you are right! Then certainly——"

"He is already turning," the little chap cut me short, and jammed his nose against the window-glass, so as to be able to see better.

I grabbed him by the neck and pulled him away, as my blood rushed to my head.

"What? What is it you are saying? Is he turning—good God in heaven—yes, it's true—he really *is* turning, all the time turning—now his broadside swings round towards us, now his stern—he has turned—he is departing. He has not seen us, he has not seen us!"

I remember that once, when I was a little boy, I got a roe-deer as a present.

I loved it a great deal and we were inseparable. It had to sleep on a rug by my bed. One beautiful summer's day we were playing in the sun on a large lawn before the house when suddenly a large, unknown hound came rushing towards my little pet and blood-

A DAY OF TERROR

thirstily chased it around the lawn. The nasty dog was about to run it down when my pet, with a shrill shriek, appealed for help. I was standing paralyzed in terror and could not get a word through my lips, when unexpectedly the owner called the dog back with a whistle. Then I threw myself, with great exultation, down alongside my pet, pressed it to my heart, kissed its black snoot, and cried and laughed with joy.

Those were my feelings now, when, with my own eyes, I saw the impossible —that the destroyer, without suspecting our presence, had steered away from us. Was it possible that he did not see us, when, according to my estimation, he was only about eight hundred meters away? Could the mate be right, and the foolish destroyer have only searched the passage in accordance with his schedule? "But," I thought, with a shiver, "how easily would not perchance a glance in our direction have betrayed us?"

Radiant with joy, I told the crew in the "Centrale" what a happy turn the affairs had taken at the last moment. A burden must have fallen from the hearts of my splendid, brave boys.

I then revealed my plans to the engineer:

"We are going to lie here until the destroyer reaches the other end of his patrol, which is about three to four sea miles from here. Then, at once, quickly empty all the tanks so that the boat cuts loose from the reef. At top speed, we will make for deep water and then dive again to a safe position below the surface."

A DAY OF TERROR

Again a light rain-cloud floated slowly towards us and favored our plans. Soon the destroyer could be seen only as a fading figure in the mist. Now we could risk to arise and get away from our other danger—the fiercely rolling breakers.

The valves were quickly opened. At once the boat came up. The terrific jolting ceased. The hand of the manometer moved upwards, and, after a few seconds, the boat's broad, dripping back broke through the surface.

There is the buoy! Now full speed ahead! We'll be soon there—now but a few hundred meters more and then the game is ours—a game on which life and death depended; a game which would have turned our hair white if we had not been so young, and if we had not, through horrible dangers, been united by true and faithful bonds.

As soon as we had placed ourselves on the right side of the longed-for buoy we again hurled ourselves deep down into the cool sea as happily as a fish which for a long time had been on dry land, and suddenly gets into its own element again.

The first and most dangerous part of our journey through the "Witch-Kettle" was over, although not without its horrible experiences. The narrow inlet was passed and also the several sea miles, wide and free from reefs and other navigation difficulties. Thus we merrily glided about in the deep and, in good spirits, hammered and listened and felt our splendid, hard-tried, heavily-tested boat all over back and forth, to see if it had pulled through without a

A DAY OF TERROR

leak from the pit of the rolling breakers; and we soon all forgot. As long as the nerves were at a continuous tension we had no time to think about past events. And though we had happily passed through and over mines and reefs, still the day was far from ended, and our main task was still before us.

This day continually brought us new and unexpected surprises, so that, at last, we had a gruesome feeling that everything had united itself for our destruction. First there were the trawlers; then the motor boats, which in pairs, with a steel net between them, searched through the channel where they suspected that U-boats were lurking. Every time we stuck up our periscope cautiously in order to look around a bit, it never failed that we had one of those searching parties right in front of us, so that we must submerge in a hurry to a greater depth in order not to be caught by the dangerous nets. And if for a short time there was an opportunity to scan the horizon undisturbed, then the atmosphere was thick, and we were unable to locate the shores, which we knew were close at hand, so that at last we hardly knew where we were, as the currents in these parts could not be estimated. Since the famous buoy we had not seen any mark which would in any degree assist us to locate ourselves.

We kept to our course up the center of the channel and trusted that our lucky star would lead us straight. Every half hour we came up from the safety of the deep and tried to take our bearings and then submerged again, dis-

A DAY OF TERROR

appointed. The crew, of course, must remain at the diving stations uninterruptedly.

About two o'clock the cook came around with pea-soup and pork in small tin cups. He also stretched up his arms to us in the conning tower with a steaming plate in his hands. I put the plate on my knees and dipped out its contents, thinking "The wild beasts are fed." The moisture, which forms in large drops on the ceiling during long trips under the water, fell down on my head and into my plate and left small splotches of oil in the pea-soup as a sign they were real drops of U-boat sweat.

We again arose to the periscope level at four o'clock. At a distance of five hundred meters, a scouting fleet was moving about. At the same time on our starboard bow a French torpedo boat with four funnels was cruising around.

I had a desire to fire a shot at this enemy, but the fact that such a shot would send the whole lurking fleet at us restrained me.

I have to admit that it was hard to hold back from taking the chance, and it was with a heavy heart that I gave orders to dive again. But this, however, saved us. If we had traveled at the periscope level for only a few minutes more, I would not be sitting here to-day, smoking my cigar and writing down the story of our adventures.

We were submerging, and the manometer showed seventeen meters. Then, suddenly, it was as if some one had hit each one of us at the same minute with a hammer. We all were unconscious for a second and found ourselves on the

A DAY OF TERROR

floor or thrown prone in some corner with our heads, shoulders, and other parts of our bodies in great pain. The whole boat shook and trembled. Were we still alive or what had happened? Why was it so dark all around us? The electric lights had gone out.

"Look to the fuse!"

"It's gone!"

"Put in the reserve fuse!"

Suddenly we had our lights again. All this happened within a few seconds and more quickly than I can tell it.

What had happened? Was it true we were lost? Would the water rush into the ship and pull us to the bottom? It must be a mine—a violent mine detonation had shaken us close by the boat. And the U-202? What were the consequences of this to the U-boat?

The reports came from all quarters:

"The bow compartment is tight!"

"The stern compartments tight!"

"The engine room all safe!"

Then the boat unexpectedly began to list. The bow sunk, and the stern arose. The ship careened violently, although the diving rudder was set hard against this.

"Herr Captain," Gröning, who was in charge of the diving rudder, shouted, "something has happened. The boat does not obey the rudder. We must have gotten hooked into some trap—a line or maybe a net. It's hell. That's all that's needed. We are jammed into some net, and all around us the mines are lining it. It's enough to set you crazy."

"Listen," I called down. "We must go through it. Put the diving rudder

A DAY OF TERROR

down hard! Both engines full speed ahead! On no condition must we rise! We must stay down at all costs. All around above us are mines!"

The engines were going at top speed. The boat shot upwards and then bent down, ripped into the net, jerked, pulled and tore and tore until the steel net gave way from the force of the attack.

"Hurrah! We are through it! The boat obeys her diving rudder!" Gröning called out from below. "The U-202 goes on her way!"

"Down, keep her down all the time. Dive to a depth of fifty meters," I commanded. "This is a horrible place—a real hell!"

I bent forward and put my head into my hands. It was rocking as if being hit by a trip hammer. My forehead ached as if pricked with needles and my ears buzzed so that I had to press my fingers into them.

"It's a horrible place," I repeated to myself. "And what luck we had, what a peculiar chance and wonderful escape that we got out at all!"

It took some time for my aching head to remember chronologically what had happened. Yes, it certainly was lucky that we, at the right moment, had submerged deep. We had been at a depth of about seventeen meters when our prow collided with the net, and the detonation followed. The more I thought of it, the plainer everything became to me.

As we had run against the net, it had stretched and that had set off the mine. The mines are set in the nets at the height at which the U-boats generally

A DAY OF TERROR

travel, which is the periscope level. If we had tried to attack the torpedo boat or, for any other reason, had remained for a few minutes more at the periscope level, we would have run into the net at a point where our enemies had hoped we would—namely, so that the mine would have exploded right under us. Now the mine, on the contrary, exploded above us, and its entire strength went in the direction where the natural resistance was smallest—which was upwards. Without causing us any greater damage than a fright and a few possible scars on the thin metal parts, which might have scratched the paint, we had escaped.

Undoubtedly the Frenchman was filled with exultation over our destruction when, waiting at his post by the net, he heard and saw the explosion, and probably reported by wireless to the entire world:

"Enemy U-boat caught and destroyed in a net by a mine explosion."

And little I begrudge him that joy if he, as a return favor in the future, will leave us alone, because we had gotten pretty nearly all we wanted, as it was.

The day's experiences were far from ended. First Engineer Krüger appeared on the stairway to the conning tower with a troubled look.

"Herr Captain," he reported, "we must have gotten something in the propeller. Our electric power is being consumed twice as fast as it should. I suppose that pieces of the metal net have entangled themselves in the blades. The laboring of the engines is terrific and

A DAY OF TERROR

the charge in the batteries is being rapidly reduced, and they are becoming exhausted."

Were we now going to have this difficulty, too! We had already consumed a large quantity of the current, because we had been compelled to dive at our highest speed and this uses up the batteries fast.

"How far can we go on it now, Herr Krüger?"

The engineer calculated in his notebook, shrugged his shoulders thoughtfully, and said:

"If we do not consume it any faster, it should last us for a couple of hours yet. It would be better, however, to decrease our speed a little."

I pondered this situation for a time. In about an hour the tide would turn and the current would be against us.

We would not be able to make much speed then, but, on the other hand, it would be dark, and we would probably dare to rise to the surface. The enemy undoubtedly believed we had perished and would have decreased his vigilance.

"All right," replied the engineer. "We'll stop one motor. There is no danger we will run aground. It is too deep here for that."

Consequently, we stopped one motor, and continued ahead at a reduced speed. At exactly five o'clock we came up again to look around. Hard by in our wake was the French torpedo boat steaming at a distance of about two hundred meters.

"Well, what is it now?" I said to the mate, and bit nervously on my lower lip. "It looks as if that rascal was after us."

A DAY OF TERROR

"It must be a coincidence," answered the unperturbed optimist.

We submerged once more, but came up again after another half hour.

The torpedo boat still came after us, steaming along in our wake at a distance of two hundred meters.

"If this is a coincidence, Mate, then it is a very, very peculiar one," I said to him.

When it was six o'clock we again took a look around. The Frenchman was still after us at the same distance.

"The devil! This is no coincidence! I'll be hanged if this is a coincidence. This is intentional. We are certanly pursued!"

There must be something the matter with us. The enemy must be able to follow us—there must be some sign that enables him to follow us even when submerged to a great depth. What could it be?

I was pondering this impossible problem. The only thing I could think of was that when the mine exploded, it had caused a leakage in one of our oil tanks and that the escaping oil left a plain trail that betrayed our presence. It was impossible at any rate on account of our slow speed under the water, against the current, that by a coincidence and without knowing about it, the Frenchman kept coming after us at the same precise distance. I had to find out about it. We submerged once more, changed our course, and proceeded at full speed. If the Frenchman had really been able to see anything of us, then he would also follow us now when we changed our course and were going four times as fast.

A DAY OF TERROR

At half past six I looked astern through the periscope and again saw, just as at five, half past five, and six, the Frenchman who, at the same speed on a changed course, continued to follow us.

VII

A LIVELY CHASE

THE fact that the French destroyer continually followed us at the same distance made me certain. There was no doubt about it. We had been discovered and were pursued. Soon the Frenchman would call for aid and would have all the bloodhounds of the sea on our scent and following us. By this time our storage batteries had begun to be exhausted, and the water was a hundred meters deep so that it was impossible for us to lie on the bottom.

"Nice prospects," I thought to myself. To the mate and crew in the "Cen-

A LIVELY CHASE

trale," I called loudly so that all could hear me:

"Well, now we have gotten rid of him at last. Didn't I say it was only a coincidence?"

I wanted to relieve the tension on the nerves of the men, because I knew how they had gone on for days at a high pitch of excitement.

In my plans, I had counted on the darkness, which must come soon. We would be very economical of the power, so that it would take us to the point which I had selected after carefully studying the chart. We kept to the same course for half an hour. Then, when the darkness must have settled down, I turned off at an angle of ninety degrees, and headed straight for the coast, where I knew the depth would permit us to rest on the bottom, to wait until the enemy had given up his manhunt. This would be towards morning, I thought, especially if the storm coming up from the southwest should increase in violence so that the searching of the water with nets would become very difficult.

The point that I had selected for our resting place was far from comfortable. And it was marked on the chart, not with the reassuring "Sd." which indicated a sand bottom, but with the dreaded "St." which meant the bottom was stony. But we had no choice. And when the devil is in a pinch, he will eat flies, although he is accustomed to better food. We did not rise again, since we knew it was dark over the sea, but continued at a considerable depth without incident and slowly approached our goal.

A LIVELY CHASE

About midnight, according to my calculations, we would be able to touch the bottom. And the storage batteries had to last up to that time. Krüger figured and figured and came to the conclusion that they would hardly last long enough.

Until ten o'clock we had heard our friend's propellers over us several times. Thereafter all became quiet on the surface, and, relieved, I drew a deep breath. They had lost the scent. It became bearable again in the U-boat. I sat on the stairway leading to the "Centrale" and was eating sandwiches and drinking hot tea with the other officers and the rest of the crew. It was almost twelve o'clock and still we had not touched bottom. What would happen if the computation of our location was wrong? This could easily have occurred, because of the strong current and our slow speed.

Half-past twelve! Still no bottom! Engineer Krüger was nervously stamping his feet and turned out one electric light after another in order to save power. For the same reason, the electric heating apparatus had been cut off for a long time, and we were very cold.

At five minutes to one we felt a slight scraping. The motors were stopped and then we reversed them in order to decrease our speed. A slight jolt! We filled the ballast tanks and were lying on the bottom where we could wait for morning at our ease. Who thought that? He who imagined that we would have any rest was disappointed. We were lying on a rock, and the tide turned about two o'clock,

A LIVELY CHASE

and the southwest wind swept the sea fiercely.

At the beginning, it seemed as if we would be all right, down there on the "St." bottom, but we soon discovered differently—when the rolling began. There was no chance of gentle resting, as on the soft sand of the North Sea, but, instead, we banged and racked from one rock to another, so it was a wonder the boat could stand it at all.

Sometimes it sounded as if large stones were rolling on deck and, again, our boat would fall three or four meters deeper with a jolt, so that the manometer was never at rest, and we had to stand this continued rising and falling between twenty-two and thirty-eight meters.

At last, towards four o'clock, we gave it up. At some of the joints in the ship, there were small leakages, and none of us had any thought of sleeping. We, therefore, went up to the surface.

I opened the conning tower hatch and let the fresh air rush against me. I had a queer sensation. It seemed to me as if we had been buried in the deep for an eternity and had had a long, bad dream.

But we had no time to dream. The storm had not calmed, but continued in its fury, and it was not long before we in the tower were soaking wet. However, to our satisfaction, the water was much warmer than in the North Sea. We noticed that the last hours had brought us much closer to our object.

It was the Gulf Stream that was flowing by us and which, in this section, is really warm, running between two shores close together.

The night was coal black. At a great

A LIVELY CHASE

distance astern, two light-houses flashed, one white and the other red. It was easy for us to know our position. No enemy was in sight, so he must have abandoned his search as useless. Can any one understand with what relief we realized this fact? Confidently we began to look ahead to success now that, at last, the dangers of the mine fields, which had been greater than we had expected, were behind us.

The exhausted batteries were quickly recharged, in order to be ready for other emergencies, and then, with our Diesel engines running, we went out into the open ocean, away from the unfriendly shores, to get some fresh air and to rest our nerves.

When the day began to break, we were twenty sea miles out and had already re-charged the batteries with so much power that, if necessary, we could proceed for several hours under water. In the dusk of the dawn, we had a new surprise.

Gröning, who, by chance, had looked toward the bow where the outlines of our boat were becoming visible, suddenly against all rules, grabbed my arm. With mouth open, eyes staring, and an arm outstretched, he pointed toward the bow.

"What is that?"

I ran up, bent forward, and followed with my eyes in the direction in which he was pointing.

"What is that?" I asked him.

I hurried toward the bow, so as to be able to see better. The boat's whole deck, from the conning tower to the prow, looked as if it had been divided into regular squares, between which

A LIVELY CHASE

dark, indistinguishable objects were moving in snakelike lines. Near me there was such a square. I stooped down and picked up a steel cord about as thick as my finger. A net, I thought, certainly a net.

"We have the remnants of the net all over us," I shouted through the noise of the storm to Gröning. "Get the nippers, hammer, and chisel ready. As soon as it is light enough, we must go to work to cut it free."

And the thick, dark snake—what was that? It came up to starboard, slipped across the deck, and disappeared to port into the darkness. It did not take us long to find out what kind of a snake it was, and I comprehended everything fully. That persistent, mysterious pursuit by the Frenchman was at once plain. Now I understood clearly what had happened on the surface after the explosion of the mine. My heart froze when I thought how readily the enemy had been able to follow our course.

We could easily trace the snake with all its curves, as it became lighter, because it was a long cork hawser, made for the purpose of sustaining the net. This was of light cork of about the thickness of a forearm and was light brown in color.

About two hundred meters of this easily perceptible hawser were floating on the water, and gave us a tail with many curves in it. This tail, which we had been dragging after us, gave us the solution of the puzzling pursuit.

When we had torn the net, with our engines at their highest speed, a large piece of it to which the hawser was fas-

A LIVELY CHASE

tened had clung to our U-boat and, after we had submerged, the hawser was still floating on the surface and continued to drag along behind us, still floating when we had submerged to a great depth. The Frenchman, who had discovered us on account of the explosion, had observed this, and, in spite of all our twistings and turnings, could follow us easily.

It was a master work of our able sea crew to cut clear that heavy steel net. The sea became still higher and washed furiously over the deck, angered by the resistance of our little nutshell. The men were standing up to their stomachs in the white, foaming waves, and had to use all their strength to stand against their force. Full of anxiety, I sat in the conning tower with a life-saving buoy ready and followed closely with worried eyes every move of my men during their dangerous work.

All went well, and, after a half hour's hard work, we were rid of the troublesome net. The nippers, hammer, and chisel and six drenched sailors disappeared down the conning tower. Each of the six held in his numbed, wet fist a rusty piece of the net as a souvenir of the fourteenth day of April.

The sun arose as if nothing had happened. From the eastern horizon it shone over the French coast as if to say:

"I am neutral! I am neutral!"

When it got up higher in the heavens and sent its greeting to England, it shivered and hid behind a thick cloud.

What was the matter with it? What was it that destroyed the joy of the greeting of the young morning? What

A LIVELY CHASE

was it yonder that wounded its neutral heart?

A steamer approached. Thick, black clouds of smoke poured out along her wake and hung heavily over the sea. She had two high, thin mastheads, two funnels, slanting slightly toward the stern, and a light-colored hull with a high bridge. "A funny ship," we decided and submerged.

When we saw her clearly through the periscope after a while, we found out the discouraging fact that she was a hospital ship. The snow-white color, the wide green bands from the bow to the stern, and the large Red Cross on the hull and the mast tops easily identified her as such.

I was just about to turn away, as an attack upon a sacred Red Cross ship could not be thought of, when my eyes as if by magic became glued to something I could not make my brain believe, something unheard of. I called Gröning to the periscope, so that he could be sure I made no mistake. No, I was right, and, to my amazement, I saw an insolence which was new to this world. No wonder that the sun had hidden its face in order not to see this scorn and mockery of humanity. No neutral sun could shine on anything like that. Only the moon could stand such lights, although they must disgust even the moon, used to dark deeds.

The ship, which was safe under the holy flag of humanity and mercy, was loaded from bow to stern with artillery supplies, and amongst the guns and ammunition there was crowded an army of soldiers and horses. Under the protection of the colors of the flags, which they

A LIVELY CHASE

were so atrociously misusing, they were proceeding in the daylight on the way to the front.

"Such a crowd!" exclaimed Gröning, and stepped back from the periscope.

"And such a shame that we can't touch it," said I, furious, and stamped on the iron floor so that it resounded. "I would like to have gotten hold of it. Such nasty people, such hypocrites! But it can't be helped. The boat is too fast and too far away for us to head it off."

Of course, we tried and went after it at top speed for some time. But the distance became greater instead of lessening, and, with our batteries exhausted, we had to abandon the chase. Then we turned, furious and swearing, and came to the surface again after a little time.

THE ADVENTURES OF THE U-202

It was a very unpleasant feeling, after a short chase, to have to lie with exhausted batteries, and limp ahead like a lame horse. Consequently we did not attempt any new enterprise, but remained on the open water for several hours charging our storage batteries. Just as we were about through with this work, there came along an insolent trawler which started to chase us. None of us had any desire to submerge again, because the sun was shining so beautifully, and it became warmer with each minute we headed south.

As the propeller, now free from the nets with which we were fouled, could give us our best speed, we immediately began the race and hastened laughingly and in good spirits ahead. Our boat cut through the waves with such speed as it showed when it first came from its

A LIVELY CHASE

wharf. The foam made a silver-white mane for us. What did we care if we got wet? We went at top speed, and, smiling, looked at the smoking and puffing steamer behind us.

"He'll never catch us," I said to Krüger, who had come up to the conning tower to ask if we were going fast enough, or if he should try to get more speed out of our engines. "Just keep her turning at the same rate, Herr Engineer. That's sufficient. It looks now as if we were gaining," I told him.

Our pursuer seemed to realize he could not overtake us and tried to anger us in other ways. Suddenly a gun flashed and a cloud of brown smoke surrounded the small steamer for a second. Shortly after that a small shell splashed into the water about a thousand meters from us and a water spout not higher than a small tree arose from the sea.

We laughed aloud.

"Such a rotten marksman! He wants to irritate us with a shotgun. That's ridiculous."

"That's an insolence without an equal," argued Lieutenant Petersen angrily, who felt that he had been insulted in his capacity of the artillery officer aboard. "We should not submit to this outrage. May I answer him, Herr Captain?" he asked me with eyes flashing.

"Yes, you may try as far as I am concerned, Petersen, but only three shots. You can't hit him at this distance, anyway, and our shells are valuable."

Grinning with joy, Petersen hurried to the guns, leveled, aimed and fired,

A LIVELY CHASE

himself, while the water washed around him up to his waist.

"Too short to the right!" I shouted to him, after I observed the high water spout through my double marine glasses.

The next shot fell close to the steamer. It became too hot for our pursuer. He turned quickly and went back in the same direction from which he had come. But the hunting fever had gotten into our blood. We also turned and pursued the fleeing pursuer. Show us what you can do now, engines!

Shot after shot flashed, roaring from our cannon. The distance was almost too great for our range. We had to set the gun at the highest possible angle in order to have any chance of hitting him. The first shots all fell short, or to the side, but at the eighth we made a hit.

THE ADVENTURES OF THE U-202

A roaring hurrah greeted the dark-brown explosion which marked the arrival of the shell on the trawler.

In vain, the trawler sent one shot after another at us. They never came near us. On our side, however, one hit followed another, and we could see that the hostile ship was listing heavily to port, and we hoped to be able to give him his death blow, when the outlines of three of his colleagues were sighted behind and to the right and left of him, approaching at great speed. Our only chance was to turn again in order to avoid being surrounded, since too many dogs can kill the hare.

Early in the evening we submerged to keep ourselves at a safe depth. We were very tired, because we had had thirty-eight hours of work and realized, now that all the excitement was over,

A LIVELY CHASE

how the nerves began to relax. To begin with, the nerve strain showed itself by the fact we could hardly go to sleep, tired as we were. And when we did doze off at last, we had many disturbing dreams. I, myself, lay awake for hours and heard through the open doors, in the deadly quiet of the U-boat, how the men tossed about in their bunks during their sleep, talking and muttering. It was as if we were in a parrot's cage instead of a submarine. Also I lived over again during the night most of the events of the past hours. The only difference was, peculiarly enough, that I was never the fish, but always the fisherman above the surface who constantly tried to catch my own U-boat with a destroyer.

When I woke I could hardly untangle the real situation, because I saw the French Captain-Lieutenant's black-bearded face before me, when, with great joy in his small dark eyes, he said:

"Diable, il faut attraper la canaille!"

VIII

THE BRITISH BULL-DOG

IN the morning a clear, blue sky and a calm sea greeted us. The wind had abated during the night and had changed so that it came from the direction of land, and, therefore, could not disturb the sea to any great extent. In the best of spirits, well satisfied and refreshed by our breakfast, we were sitting on the conning tower, and enjoying the mild air of spring and puffing one cigarette after another. During the night we had reached the position where, for the present, we intended to make our attacks on the merchant transportation which was very flourishing in that region. We crossed the steamship lanes in all directions with guns loaded and with a sharp lookout so as not to lose any opportunity to damage the enemy's commerce.

Shortly before dinner the first merchant ship arose on the south horizon. It was a sailer, a large, full-rigged schooner, which, hard by the wind, headed towards the French coast. With majestic calm, lightly leaning to the wind, the splendid ship approached. The snow-white sails glittered in the sun in the far distance. The light, slender hull plowed sharply through the sea.

With a delighted "Hello," we hurled ourselves on our prey. Above our heads fluttered pennants and signal-flags which signified:

"Leave the ship immediately!"

THE BRITISH BULL-DOG

Sharply and distinctly in the bright sun the command traveled from our boat to the large, heavily-loaded ship, and the colors of the German flag-of-war, which floated from the mast behind the tower, left no doubt of the grim sincerity of the command.

Did they not have a signal-book over there, or did they not want to understand us? Ah! A flag went up on the main-mast. The wind unfolded it and, proudly and distinctly, France's tri-color could be seen. The flag stopped at half-mast—a distress-signal! The flag on half-mast was the pursued sailer's call for help. They understood our command and were now looking for assistance before obeying us. Wait, my little friend, we'll soon get that out of you.

"Hoist the signals: 'Stop immediately or I'll shoot!'"

The signal flew up. Now, look here, Frenchy, this is no joke; soon the little, gray animal, which is circling around you, will bite.

"We will give them three minutes to consider the matter, then we'll shoot down the masts," I said to Lieutenant Petersen, who was standing by the guns, and, in his excitement, was stepping from one foot to another.

With watch in hand, I counted three full minutes. The sailer did not take any notice of us, just as if our existence had nothing to do with him.

"Such impudence," I murmured, as I put down my watch. Soon thereafter resounded through the entire boat:

"Fire!"

"Rrrrrms!" the guns thundered with

a deafening roar, and the shell whistled through the schooner's high rigging, in which it tore a large hole, struck the mainyard of the forward mast, exploded, and snapped off the heavy mast, so that, with its sails, it fell like a broken wing on the deck of the ship.

The results were immediately apparent. The red and white pennant, which in the international language means: "I understand!" flew to the masthead. The sailors, who had gathered in groups, looked at us in alarm. They were scattered by the commands of the captain and hurried in all directions to their posts. Giving orders in the singing accents of the French language, the sails were soon lowered and the ship slowed up. The boats were swung out and made ready, and men, with life-saving buoys, were running all over in great excitement.

We closed in on the ship to windward, and I called to the captain to make haste—that I would give him just ten minutes more to get away before torpedoing his ship.

In the bow compartment, where the torpedo tubes are built into the U-boat and the torpedoes themselves are stored, there was feverish activity from the minute we saw the hostile ship and the alarm was sounded. It is cramped in the forward part of a U-boat, very cramped, and it is necessary to have a special crew of very skilled men to be able to accomplish their purpose in this network of tubes, valves, and pumps. The officers' mess, which is just back of the torpedo compartment, is quite roomy and comfortable. It was now

THE BRITISH BULL-DOG

changed in a moment to an uninhabitable place. Ready hands pulled down the oil-stained curtains in front of the bunks and folded up the narrow table and the four chairs without backs. These were all placed in a corner hurriedly, and the luxuries were all gone, making room to handle the torpedoes.

Schweckerle, in command of the torpedo tubes, was like a father in the way he watched over his torpedoes. He loved them as if they were children and continually oiled and greased them and examined them carefully. They said of him that he mourned when he had to separate himself from one of them. And I, myself, saw that when a torpedo, for some reason or other slightly turned, did not strike its target, he went around broken-hearted for many days and could not eat.

THE ADVENTURES OF THE U-202

This faithful fellow was now busily occupied taking care of his children and had selected "Flink" and "Reissteufel" (these were his names for the two torpedoes now ready for the tubes) when the command was given:

"First torpedo tube ready!"

This meant "Reissteufel" was to go.

Schweckerle was in his element and, when he gave his commands, the sailors ran as if the devil was at their heels.

"You here! You there! You take that! You take the other! Forward! Hurry! Take hold! Get the oil can! That's good! That's enough! Now put it in—push it forward! Now hold back! Slowly—slowly—stop!"

One last word of encouragement to the torpedo disappearing into the tube! At last the parting glance, and Schweckerle slammed the tube shut, and "Reissteufel" was ready to go on his way.

At once this was reported to me in the conning tower, but only a few of the allotted ten minutes had passed and we had plenty of time. We took a closer look at the sailing ship before we sent her to the bottom for good. She was a large modern ship, constructed entirely of steel, and had the latest equipment over all, even in the rigging. She could carry a cargo of from three to four thousand tons and, without doubt, had come from a long distance, because sailing ships of this size do not travel along the coast. What kind of a cargo did she carry?

The French crew stepped into her boats and left their ship. The last boat was capsized, when it was launched, and all in it fell into the sea. Another one of the boats came quickly to the rescue and picked up the swimming and struggling sailors. When all had been saved, I turned our prow toward the sailing ship, which was now lying absolutely still, and fired our first torpedo.

Poor Schweckerle! There it goes, but it heads straight, Schweckerle, true as an arrow. Bravo, Schweckerle! The French in the lifeboats, who had approached us where they believed themselves safest, yelled in terror when the detonation followed and the water spout was thrown high above the mastheads.

"Oh, mon Dieu! Mon Dieu! Notre pauvre vaisseau!"

"Poor devils," I thought. "I understand how you feel over your beautiful, fine ship, but why didn't you stay at home? Why do you go to sea when you know what threatens? Why do you

THE BRITISH BULL-DOG

or your governments force us to destroy your ships wherever we can find them? Do you think we are gong to wait until our own women and children starve and let you keep your bread baskets full before we defend ourselves? You have started it. You are responsible for the consequences. If you would discontinue your inhuman way of carrying on the war, then we would let your sailing ships and steamers pass unmolested, when they do not carry contraband. You have wanted war to the knife. Good, we have accepted your challenge."

The sailing ship sank rapidly by the stern, turning over on her side until the yard arms touched the water and the red bottom could be seen. And, at last, when the pressure burst the forward cargo hatch, there was a shower of corn, and the proud ship, with a dying gurgle, disappeared into the deep.

The captain came aboard us. He never lost for a minute his personality as a polite Frenchman with elegant manners. He swung himself into the conning tower, smiled with the pleasantry of a boulevardier, and, with a gracious bow, handed his ship's papers to "mon capitaine." In the most polite and courteous German, I offered him a cigarette, for which he thanked me with a smile, as if we had been the best of friends for years. We questioned him. From where was he coming and where bound? He answered frankly and showed us without requesting it what a valuable catch we had made. It impressed him greatly how we were traveling about in our little shell, and there was no doubt he had an inclination

THE BRITISH BULL-DOG

to go along with us on our sea-robbing voyage, if he could have done it.

When I asked him why he had not obeyed our signals to stop, he acted as innocent as a new-born baby, and assured us that he never saw our signals. Indeed, he went so far as to say he had not even observed our U-boat until we fired our gun. When I pointed out to him that he had hoisted the signal of distress long before that and that this made his story hardly believable, he dropped the subject with great skill and gave the conversation a new turn. It was impossible to catch this smooth Frenchman, and when I had him cornered so that another man would not have known what to say, he slipped through the conversation like an eel with his great politeness.

I was struck with surprise to see

his men so well dressed, washed, and shaved. I, a "barbarian," did not want to be behind the Frenchman in point of manners, so I complimented him on his crew's splendid appearance. Then he began to lament.

"Oh, my poor boys," he complained. "They have not looked so well throughout our voyage, but only to-day they have been scrubbing themselves, because they hoped to be able to get ashore tonight. See this, mon capitaine," he continued and opened his log—"on January 23rd we cleared from Saigon and have sailed nearly around the world, and now, only a few hours before reaching our port, we are met with such a disaster. What a tragedy! What a tragedy!"

I consoled him the best I could and promised to assist them so that they could land at the same time they had hoped. Then I, as he was about to leave the U-boat, offered him another cigarette, shook his hand amicably, and sent him off the ship.

We had agreed that I would tow his boats toward the coast until some new spoils hove into sight. Then they would have to do the best they could for themselves.

Soon after two o'clock, this occurred when the mastheads with the tips of white sails arose over the horizon.

We cast off from the boats, wished the Frenchman a safe journey, and turned toward our new prey, while Schweckerle made "Flink" ready.

As we came nearer, we discovered something that made us jump. We had been certain that the ship which was approaching was a large three-master, rigged somewhat like the one that we had just sunk, but what now astonished us and aroused our suspicion was that we distinctly saw, at times, dark clouds of smoke that seemed to be closely associated with the sailing ship which floated between and behind her sails.

"Anything that you cannot explain is always suspicious."

In accordance with this well tested rule for U-boats, we cautiously kept off a little, so as to let the mysterious ship pass us at some distance. We had heard too much of U-boat sinking to rush at anything blindly. What would happen if, behind the mask of the big sailing ship, a ready and fast torpedo boat was sneaking which, quick as lightning, would swoop down on us? First we must find out with what we had to deal.

We could soon make out what it was.

THE BRITISH BULL-DOG

At a distance of about two hundred meters in front of the sailer, there was a strong tug pulling the full-rigged ship with a thick hawser, so that it could make better time. There was nothing suspicious in this in these parts of the sea. It often happened that sailing ships were towed in over the final fifty miles of their voyage to reach port before evening, and thus gain an entire day. The large tugboats went far out to sea and tendered their high-priced services.

"Ah," we thought, "there is no danger here! But on the contrary, it looks like a grand chance to sink a ship, and, at the same time, send its crew ashore safely"—the thought we always had in mind when it did not interfere with our duty.

I rubbed my hands in satisfaction.

THE ADVENTURES OF THE U-202

We would give the crew of the sailing ship a chance to get aboard the tugboat and so send them home. Maybe they might also meet the shipwrecked crew of the French sailing ship and take them aboard.

At top speed we headed for the tugboat. First we circled round our prey to be sure that we would not be surprised by a masked gun and especially examined the tugboat, because he traveled back and forth daily through the danger zone, and would be more apt to be armed than would the sailing ship coming from a long voyage.

There was nothing suspicious to be seen—therefore we advanced. We approached the stern of the tugboat, slowed down, and, within calling distance, kept pace with him. Gröning, Petersen, Lohmann, and a sailor were with me in the conning tower. The tugboat flew the British flag. I shouted with the full power of my lungs:

"Take aboard the crew! Take aboard the crew!"

I waved with my left hand toward the sailing ship, in order to make my meaning clear. The commander of the "little bulldog," as Petersen called the tugboat, took his short clay pipe out of his mouth, spat far out from the bridge where he was standing in a careless attitude, but otherwise took no notice of us except that he may have thrown a shrewd, cunning glance our way. I thought he was hard of hearing and drew a little closer and yelled again:

"Take the crew off!"

The wind had increased during the last few hours and the sea began to run higher and was washing over our deck.

It was impossible for us to use our guns —the crew would have been swept away without any chance of being saved— and we were, for that reason, unable to emphasize our commands in a desirable manner, but we knew what to do when the commander on the "bulldog" did not display any inclination to comply with our ten-times repeated order. I had a revolver handed to me from below and let a bullet whistle close to the head of the stubborn rascal. The Englishman seemed to understand this language better. He abandoned his careless slouch, blew the tug's siren, and yelled loud, sharp commands to the crew. Then he turned for the first time towards me, put his hand to his cap with a short salute, and next lifted his right hand vertically in the air, which, according to the international language of sailors, meant:

THE BRITISH BULL-DOG

"I understand and will obey."

The crew on the "bulldog," which in reality bore the name *Ormea,* had, however, cast off the hawser and were now standing idly all around the deck with their hands in their pockets and looked at us curiously. The captain went to the engine telegraph and signaled "Half speed ahead."

"Ha," we thought, "now he'll turn and lay himself alongside the sailing ship."

What happened next took only a minute.

When the *Ormea* had gathered speed, it certainly turned—but not to port, which would have been the nearest way, but towards us. At the same time the skipper signaled to his engine room:

"Full speed ahead!"

The sturdily built, speedy tug rushed

at us, pushing aside the waves with her prow.

We had, of course, been keenly observing every move made on the tugboat, but suspected nothing until that moment when he headed straight for us.

"The man is crazy!" I yelled. "He intends to ram us. Full speed with both engines. Hard a-starboard!"

But it looked as if we had grasped the situation too late. The tug had gotten a start on us in speed and came at us, smoking copiously, like a mad bulldog. The distance between us, which to begin with had been two hundred meters, decreased with great rapidity. Now the prow was hardly fifty meters from us. Our hair stood on end.

"Bring up pistols and guns," I called down.

These weapons, which were hanging

THE BRITISH BULL-DOG

always loaded, were quickly handed up to us, and we opened a quick fire on our onrushing enemy. Already I saw the captain's sly, water-blue eyes scornfully glittering and read the spiteful joy in his grinning face. He had good reason to feel happy. He would reach us, he must reach us, because he had greater speed than we had, and his position was more advantageous. Nearer and nearer came the moment when would stick his blunt, steel prow into our side, and the nearer he approached, the harder our hearts beat.

Twenty meters—fifteen meters! Was there no escape—no hope of rescue?

Yes! Gröning, the calm and thoughtful Gröning, became our savior. He was on one knee by me on the conning tower platform and sent one shot after another at the oncoming target. Suddenly he caught the idea which saved us.

"The helmsman!" he yelled. "All men aim at the helmsman!"

In the pilot house with glass windows, stood the mate of the *Ormea* by his wheel with a sinister grin searching for the point where the blow would be most deadly. We saw him distinctly as he stood there.

Action followed immediately on Gröning's saving thought. We stopped the wild shooting against the dangerous prow, and all of us aimed at the helmsman and fired. Hardly had the first volley been discharged when we heard a shriek, and the Englishman threw his arms high and fell forward over his wheel. As he fell, he gripped the spoke of the wheel and spun it around. This saved us from our great-

THE BRITISH BULL-DOG

est danger. The prow which was to have crushed us was only about three meters distant when the tug was thrown hard aport, so that it hit only the air.

To show how close the tug was to us, as it swung, its stern struck our diving tank and left a scar as a remembrance. As the beast of prey after missing does not attempt another leap, so the tugboat put on full speed in an effort to escape. The whistling of our bullets and the loss of his mate had apparently made a coward out of a little tugboat captain, but we gave him credit for having been resourceful, after we had recovered from the excitement of the moment and recalled all the circumstances.

I quietly pressed Gröning's hand and smilingly touched the spot on his breast, there just below his brave, fearless heart, a spot which, in accordance with the command of his Majesty, the Kaiser, should be reserved for the reward due such a hero. To-day that place is decorated with the black, silver framed Iron Cross.

IX

HOMEWARD BOUND!

WHY should I continue relating events which were coupled with less danger and were less remarkable than those we had already experienced and which I have already carefully described? The climax of the journey was reached at the encounter with the *Ormea,* and, after the climax is reached, one should be brief. For those interested, I can assure them that we did not let the schooner escape which had tried to save herself by flight, but hurried quickly after her, and, as soon as the crew had disembarked, torpedoed her. However, we regretted that the captain of the tug that tried to ram us escaped through her superior speed.

We were fortunate enough to make another catch on this same day, just as darkness was setting in, a steamer loaded with meat, inward bound from Sydney. We continued for several days through this fruitful field of operation in every direction and had both good and bad luck. Schweckerle had to bite into a bitter apple several times, as one after another of his children faithlessly abandoned him. But he had the joy of knowing that none of them went contrary to his good bringing-up and the care it had received.

Many successes we put down in our log and sometimes exciting episodes and narrow escapes, when our enemy's destroyers and patrol ships came across our path of daily toil, so that we should

HOMEWARD BOUND!

not be too presumptuous and careless.

Then at last came the day when we decided to start our homeward journey. The torpedoes and shells were exhausted. Of oil, fresh water, and provisions we had such a scanty supply left that it was necessary for us to return. It was impossible to tell what kind of weather we would have on our return trip, and, if it did not storm, there might be strong head winds to hold us back.

I decided to take a new route for our journey home. The Witch-Kettle with its horrors was still fresh in our minds and we preferred to take a roundabout way, rather than to run risks which could be easily avoided after a successfully completed task. In this period of thirteen days our nerves had been affected and there was little power of resistance left in them. It would not be advisable to put them to another severe test.

So it came to pass on the fifteenth day after the start of the voyage, that a great storm hit us and for several days kept us hard at work. We found ourselves far up in the North Atlantic where the warm spring for a long time still wears its winter's furs, and the sun never rises high. The icy, north wind, which blows three-quarters of the year, would in any event devour all his warmth.

Repentantly, we had again picked up our thick camel's wool garments which we had laid off in the southern waters. The further we went north, the heavier the clothes that we donned.

In addition to the cold there came a storm, the like of which I had never seen

HOMEWARD BOUND!

during my entire service on the sea, and to describing which I will devote a few lines, because a storm on a U-boat is altogether different from a storm at sea in any other vessel.

The barometer had been uncertain for two days. Its hasty rising and falling in accordance with the changes of the atmosphere made us suspect we would soon get rough weather. It was the night between April twenty-fourth and twenty-fifth. We traveled submerged to a considerable depth, and I was lying in my bunk asleep, partly undressed. At about two o'clock I was awakened and received the report:

"Lieutenant Petersen asks that the Captain-Lieutenant kindly come to the 'Centrale,' as it is impossible for him to steer the boat any longer alone."

I threw on my jacket and hurried for

the stern. On my way, on account of the heavy rolling of the boat, I realized what was the trouble. There must be a terrific storm above accompanied by a sea which only the Atlantic could stir up.

Lieutenant Petersen confirmed my opinion of the conditions which had developed during the night and added that he had never had so much trouble with the diving rudder before in his life. This meant a great deal, for Petersen was with me when our U-boat had been equipped for service for the first time, and had already gone through all kinds of weather. In spite of all the watchfulness that he and the well-trained crew used, the diving rudder's pressure was not powerful enough to resist the enormous strength of the waves. The boat was tossed up and down as if she had no rudder whatever. Only after we had submerged twice as deep as we had been were we able to steady the boat to any degree. We could still feel the force of the sea and knew the storm must be terrific.

When, at daybreak, we arose to the surface there was no chance to open the hatches. The opal green mountains of waves came rolling and foaming at us. They smothered the boat with the great masses of water, washed completely over the deck and even up over the tower. If any one had dared to open the hatch and go out on the conning tower, he would certainly have been lost. I was standing at the periscope and observed the wrath of the elements. It seemed as if we were in a land of mountains which the U-boat had to climb, only to be suddenly hurled down again.

THE ADVENTURES OF THE U-202

I could see only so far as the next ridge, which always seemed to be even higher than the last, and if there had been any chance of seeing more, it would have been impossible in the flying foam and spray. The rain whipped the water violently and darkened the sky so that it was like dusk. The boat worked itself laboriously through the heavy sea. The joints cracked and trembled when the boat slid down from the peak of a wave to be buried in the deep trough.

We had to cling to some oil-soaked object in order not to be tossed about. Through the strain put on the body by the terrible rolling of the boat, by the damp, vaporous air, and by lack of sleep and food, we finally became exhausted, but at this time we had no desire to eat. The storm continued for three days and nights without abating. Then the sky cleared, the wind dropped, and the sea became calmer. At noon of the third day the sun broke through the clouds for the first time. Shortly before this, we had dared open the conning tower hatch and greeted the rays of the sun, although we had to pay for this pleasure with a cold bath.

We had been drifting about for three days without knowing our location. No wonder we greeted our guide with great joy, and quickly produced the sextant to find out where we were. Our calculations showed that, during the entire time, we had been circling around in one spot and had not gotten one mile nearer our port. But what did that matter? The storm was abating, the sea was calming down, and our splendid, faithful boat had stood the test once more, and, in spite of all storms, had survived.

We reached the North Sea the next afternoon and could change our course to the south with happy hearts. Every meter, every mile, every hour brought us nearer home. No one who has not, himself, experienced this home-coming can understand the joy that fills a U-boat sailor's heart when, after a successful voyage, he sees the coast of his fatherland; or when he turns the leaves of his log and, astonished, reads the scrawled lines which tell fairy tales of the dangers and joys and asks himself:

"Have you really gone through all that?"

Who can understand the joy of a commander's heart when, sitting by his narrow writing table, he is carefully working out his report to his superiors?

HOMEWARD BOUND!

"Have sunk X steamers—X sailing ships."

All around me were the happy faces of the crew. All were satisfied, every danger past and forgotten, thanks to the strength of youth and their stout hearts.

April 30—Nine-thirty A. M.

The lead was thrown. Now the water became shallow, for we are going into the bay—the German bay.

"It's twenty-four meters deep," reported Lohmann, who in his feverish desire to get ashore had been up on the conning tower since four o'clock, although he should really have been off watch at eight. He wanted to be the first one to sight land, because he is proud of his fine eyesight and was as happy as a child when he discovered something before his commander did.

"The lead shows twenty-four!"

"See if it agrees with the chart," I called to the mate who sat in the conning tower with the chart on his knee.

"It agrees exactly," the mate called back, after he had compared the measurement by the lead with the depth that was marked on the chart where we estimated we were.

"How far is it to land?"

"Eight and a half miles."

In five more minutes, the German islands of the North Sea arose before our eyes. Now we were unable to restrain ourselves further. We tore off our caps and waved them exultantly, greeting our home soil with a roaring hurrah. Our cheer penetrated into the boat, from stern to prow, and even set

HOMEWARD BOUND!

Schweckerle's heart on fire, where he was sitting alone and idle amongst the torpedo cradles.

Shortly thereafter we glided into the mouth of the river with the pennant bearing our name proudly fluttering from the masthead. This told all the ships that met us:

"Here comes U-boat 202!"

All knew by our announcement that we were returning from a long voyage and we were greeted with an enthusiastic and noisy reception. Officers and men thronged the decks, and in our inmost hearts we appreciated the great cheer:

"Three cheers for his Majesty's U-202! Hurrah! Hurrah! Hurrah!"

Thus the proud German high seas fleet received our little roughly-used boat.

THE ADVENTURES OF THE U-202

At three o'clock on the afternoon of April 30 U-202 dropped her anchor in the U-boat harbor.

www.ingramcontent.com/pod-product-compliance
Lightning Source LLC
Chambersburg PA
CBHW011950150426
43195CB00018B/2883